Palgrave Studies in Creativity and Culture

Series Editors
Vlad Petre Glăveanu
School of Psychology
Dublin City University
Dublin, Ireland

Brady Wagoner (iD)
Communication and Psychology
Aalborg University
Aalborg, Denmark

Both creativity and culture are areas that have experienced a rapid growth in interest in recent years. Moreover, there is a growing interest today in understanding creativity as a socio-cultural phenomenon and culture as a transformative, dynamic process. Creativity has traditionally been considered an exceptional quality that only a few people (truly) possess, a cognitive or personality trait 'residing' inside the mind of the creative individual. Conversely, culture has often been seen as 'outside' the person and described as a set of 'things' such as norms, beliefs, values, objects, and so on. The current literature shows a trend towards a different understanding, which recognises the psycho-socio-cultural nature of creative expression and the creative quality of appropriating and participating in culture. Our new, interdisciplinary series Palgrave Studies in Creativity and Culture intends to advance our knowledge of both creativity and cultural studies from the forefront of theory and research within the emerging cultural psychology of creativity, and the intersection between psychology, anthropology, sociology, education, business, and cultural studies. Palgrave Studies in Creativity and Culture is accepting proposals for monographs, Palgrave Pivots and edited collections that bring together creativity and culture. The series has a broader focus than simply the cultural approach to creativity, and is unified by a basic set of premises about creativity and cultural phenomena.

Pier Paolo Bellini

The Creative Gesture

Contexts, Processes, Actors of Creativity

Pier Paolo Bellini
SUSeF
University of Molise
Campobasso, Italy

ISSN 2755-4503   ISSN 2755-4511   (electronic)
Palgrave Studies in Creativity and Culture
ISBN 978-3-031-54218-3   ISBN 978-3-031-54219-0   (eBook)
https://doi.org/10.1007/978-3-031-54219-0

This Palgrave Macmillan imprint is published by the registered company Springer Nature Switzerland AG.
The registered company address is: Gewerbestrasse 11, 6330 Cham, Switzerland

Paper in this product is recyclable.

To the friends and colleagues who have made this work "imaginable."
To the young scholars with whom I have collaborated over these years who made me see the creative force at work within the research.
To scholars ahead of me, Prof. Guido Gili, who taught me about communication, and Prof. Giovanni Maddalena, who taught me about gesture.
To the international colleagues who forced me to discuss.
To my family who forced me to be all-around creative.

Contents

1

Nature and Sources of Creativity

Abstract "The progress of civilisation is essentially attributable to creative thinking" (Kemple and Nissenberg, Early Childhood Education Journal, 2000, p. 67). The framework within which the creative capacity proper to the human species is nowadays read is decidedly "positive": it is very rare to come across "negative" readings, if not in a generally ironic sense (linked to "creative interpretations" of laws, morals, responsibility, etc.). Yet, this was not always the case. In this chapter, I will focus on the reconstruction of a historical-cultural framework that has also seen the social prestige of this energy change considerably, after which I will look at its theoretical categorizations, its practical and symbolic operational dynamics, and its relationship with intelligence. This introductory framework will allow us to enter more consciously into the specific investigation of this volume, namely the in-depth study of the social dimensions of this individual and collective capacity.

The author of this volume is a sociologist of cultural processes: the structural perspective therefore, with regard to both authors of reference and research methodology, is sociological. He wanted, however, to attempt the impervious and sometimes slippery road of "disciplinary contamination" for several reasons: (a) creativity, like all human realities and perhaps to a greater extent, overflows every disciplinary embankment; (b) to really learn something about creativity, it is necessary to come to terms with as many disciplines as possible that involve or have been involved by it and acknowledge that some (in this case, psychology)

© The Author(s) 2024   1
P. P. Bellini, *The Creative Gesture*, Palgrave Studies in Creativity and Culture,
https://doi.org/10.1007/978-3-031-54219-0_1

possess an investigative history of incomparable depth; (c) the fertile ground of creativity (we shall see) is curiosity: as children are well aware, curiosity and a receptive mind will push ajar many doors behind which can be glimpsed concepts, novelties, ideas for which our eyes and minds are not yet equipped. It is a risk worth taking.

Keywords Paradigm • Transcendence • Symbolic combination • Intelligences

1.1   Story of a Great Return

Creativity is back on the agenda! Widely discussed and debated once again, it has indisputably returned to being à la page, and its language has spread "from the narrow world of specialists to the everyday life of ordinary people" (Melucci 1994a, p. 12).

The unequivocal proof of this return can be seen in the increase in the number of creative consulting agencies and in-house creativity departments, the surge in "how-to" books (see Jaussi and Dionne 2003), the expansion of research, the creation of institutes, and applications in the organizational field. This is mainly because economists are definitely looking at creativity as a form of capital, but also and above all "as an engine of economic growth and social dynamism" (McWilliam and Dawson 2008, p. 635).

In short, being creative today pays off. It is in the world of big business, in fact, that cultural models in which creativity is perceived as a value of high social desirability are elaborated; "the new mantra is 'be creative'; change and the new are values and we must continually adapt to them" (Finney Botti 1994, p. 101).

The big companies themselves are the trailblazers of change and renewal: the capitalists who command today are no longer the owners of "hard" structures, of mines, ports, steel plants, or car factories. Zygmunt Bauman observed that in the current list of the richest Americans, only a very low percentage are industrialists; the rest are financiers, lawyers, doctors, scientists, architects, programmers, designers, and all sorts of celebrities from the worlds of entertainment, television, and sports. The largest fortunes are found in invention, communication, marketing gimmicks, and in entertainment; in other words, in new ideas. It is the people with brilliant ideas "who nowadays inhabit the rooms of the upper floors. The main resources of which capital is made [...] are knowledge, inventiveness, imagination, the ability to think and the courage to think differently—qualities that universities were invited to create, disseminate and instill" (Bauman 2012, p. 57).

In the light of the above, it has been observed that this phenomenon has upset the classic analytical categories of sociology, a process that has recently led to the emergence of a new class, the "creative class." Its members are identified as "producers of creativity," and as this is the real driving element behind economic development, "in our society they have become, in terms of influence, the dominant class" (Florida 2002, It. trans. 2003, p. 3). Result: "In the past few decades, creativity has become rather like money: everyone seems to want more of it" (Briskman 2009, p. 17).

That said, it is still true that the value of the creative attitude, once again now held in esteem and sought after, goes well beyond the immediate utility of its instrumental applications. Creativity, as we will see, is a dynamism that has to do with the very expression of human action, identity, values, and social and civil achievements: it is therefore now considered "fundamental for our survival" (Richards 2007) and "necessary for our process of consciousness" (Lindqvist 2003).

It is perhaps due to these insights that recent studies dedicated to this topic have progressively expanded to various sectors of human expressiveness and work, where the positive contribution of creativity to academic performance, violence prevention, and overall success in life is increasingly evident. This interest is based on the assumption that creativity is an indispensable skill in an increasingly complex, uncertain, and changing world: this could be the reason that an increasing number of countries have emphasized the "developing students' creative potential in education policies" (Hernández-Torrano and Ibrayeva 2020, p. 1) and that "even the lowest workers are nowadays pressed to display creativity and originality" (Reuter 2015, p. 18).

Although the phenomenon can be investigated scientifically, such studies nonetheless come up against an impasse: we, too, in our investigation of creativity, will have to face this aspect that eludes analytical strategies and will be obliged to define creativity as a "mysterious continent of the spirit," a kind of "disconcerting tension" that we carry within us and that always "pushes us to adjust nature with culture, so that the world we leave our children will be different to the world we inherited from our fathers" (De Masi 2003, p. 15).

1.2   Creativity as a "Subject of Study"

Generally speaking, creativity has received relatively little academic attention compared to the broader mental faculty referred to as "intelligence": this may be partly due to cultural reasons and partly to the difficulty in understanding what exactly the object of the study is and especially "in defining and measuring the creativity dependent variable" (Batey et al. 2010, p. 532).

Things started to change in the middle of the last century: sector studies were very few and far between until Joy Paul Guilford (1950), then president of the American Psychological Association, pointed out in a now historic speech that there was "little research on creativity relative to the importance of such research to the field of psychology" (Sternberg 2005, p. 370) and the little that there was, was pitiful.

We will now delve into the evolution of the human sciences: in order to have a clearer understanding of the uncertainty that plagued the methodology of the time, it is useful to try to clarify the ancestral "cultural motivations." First of all, it must not be forgotten that the semantic root of the term creativity refers to an action that, in the millennial religious tradition, was the exclusive prerogative of God: only the divine, in fact, is capable of "bringing into being" from nothing, or, in other words, "creating." Man, even at the peak of his expressiveness, can merely transform reality, "perfecting" what already exists; indeed, until a few centuries ago, the concept that man could be creative in thought and action was considered blasphemous. In the narrative of the Old Testament, creation took place over six days: a process, therefore, in time. However, tradition offers us the conception of a static, finished, complete, and closed creation: and so, men "were not given the idea that Creation could be perpetually open" (Anderson 1959, It. trans. 1972, p. 12), constantly available for change, for a new creative gesture.

Things were no different in the culture of ancient Greece, as the myths remind us: the story of Prometheus is a warning to "creative spirits" about the possible consequences of their actions. When Prometheus stole fire—a metaphor for the creative spark—from the gods to give it to the people, "he enraged Zeus and received his punishment" (Glăveanu 2018, p. 26).

Precisely because of its mysterious analogy with the divine, in Western cultural tradition the "creative" quality was attributed exclusively to certain individuals: the prophet, the haruspex, the seer, the creative genius as the artist. In other words, it was assigned to those roles that were socially charged with penetrating the deep mysteries of reality. Only a few were allowed to intuit and transcendentally manifest the real, the beautiful, Nature, or the "spirit."

A synthesis of a systematic reflection by Vlad Glăveanu, a psychologist at the University of Dublin, may help in the onerous task of analyzing the development of the concept of creativity. Glăveanu proposes an effective three-phase paradigm that can be integrated with the contributions of other international researchers. As he himself specifies, the historical progression implicit in his reconstruction does not exclude that "instances" of these paradigms coexist at different times and are certainly interwoven in today's scientific landscape.

1.2.1 The "He" Paradigm

This is the so-called phase of genius, more precisely, of the lone genius. The emphasis (common, after all, both to the Renaissance and the Romantic conception) is on the exceptionality of individuals who are capable of the act of creation and on the consequent and frequent "disconnection" from the rest of their environment: only a few are chosen to be creative and those who are must stand out from the masses. Consequently, the creator detaches himself from the community "and, by this, ends up building a pathological image of him/her" (Glăveanu 2010, p. 80).

This vision (which, often arrogantly, we tend to define as "romantic" and therefore obsolete, outdated) has represented not a few obstacles to the affirmation of a "modern" concept of creativity and continues to leave residues in unexpected places: even today, a good number of scientists believe that creativity "is not subject to rules or methods," and therefore one cannot learn to be creative. In reality, as some important case studies have shown, innovative discoveries result from highly structured rational processes: the fact that sometimes even great scientists invoke sudden flashes of intuition to explain their creative work is not in itself a decisive factor, since "many scientists adhere to the romantic view of creativity themselves, and hence, their recollections are colored through that view" (Meheus and Nickles 2000, p. 234). On the other hand, it should be kept in mind that the high levels of technicality and specialist knowledge, required for scientific discovery and the extreme complexity of the processes involved, make it difficult even for creative scientists themselves to explain their achievements rationally and describe the path used to attain them.

While in the sixteenth and seventeenth centuries discovery was seen as an integral part of a methodology (it was believed that there was a "logic of discovery," a set of rules that when properly applied led to new and interesting discoveries), things changed significantly in the romantic era. Creative products could derive from genius, from the illuminations of intuition, or chance, from a "leap," a "breakthrough," but not from the simple application of method.

However, these two different conceptions converge on the common ground of "exceptionality." Then again, it should be noted that "genius," in the strict sense of the term, is a phenomenon that is still difficult to explain today and it cannot be excluded that genetic differences are involved: certainly, great geniuses (especially in certain fields, such as music or mathematics) "seem to be born with talents that cannot be explained solely by learning or the environment alone" (Nakamura and Csikszentmihalyi 2003, p. 190).

At a certain point, however, a number of factors intervened to promote the urgent need of new investigative paradigms for the analysis of creativity. We shall examine three of these in detail.

The first was an increasing awareness of the fact that individual creative ability is certainly a result of personality-related factors (cognitive style and skills) but that, more properly, it should be considered as a complex emergence of "relevant task domain expertise, motivation and social and contextual influences" (Shalley and Gilson 2004, p. 36). Contextual factors, therefore, interact with individual characteristics and influence creative performance.

The second factor was the advent of the concept of "motion," characteristic of Darwinian theory, based on the idea of something that was not absolute, definitively stabilized, "of something that could emerge, evolve and yet have infinity as its goal" (Anderson 1959, It. trans. 1972, p. 13). Then, with the process of "disenchantment" (to use a Weberian category), a paradigm was established in which "the ability to solve problems and arouse emotions" (Federici 2006, p. 18) seems to prevail as an essential element: from heaven to earth.

In the 1970s and 1980s, a large group of researchers shifted their focus from personality to process given the acquired awareness that "the social processes concerning creativity have rarely been studied" (Schepers van der Berg 2007, p. 408); such processes, they claimed, could clarify the dynamics underlying creativity more effectively than the research conducted so far on its so-called individual predictors (such as personality traits).

This shift from a focus on personality and individual differences to those mental processes that underlie "not only exceptional abilities, but also everyday problem-solving and decision-making skills" (Sawyer 2003, p. 5) led to the third factor that definitively took over the field of subsequent scientific research: creativity as the ability of the "man in the street," as daily energy and strategy in dealing with routine matters.

This led to the emergence of a new paradigm.

1.2.2 The "I" Paradigm

The paradigm of "I," the self, replaces the genius with the "normal" person. This can be defined as the "democratization" of creativity: everyone is capable of creativity since "it is no longer a capacity of the few chosen by God, biology or unique psychological features" (Glăveanu 2010, p. 81).

It was Joy Paul Guilford who first drew the attention of psychologists to the topic of the creative personality, so giving rise to a new perspective of investigation, a perspective thanks to which creative acts can be expected (regardless of their scope or frequency), "from almost all individuals" (Guilford 1950, p. 446).

It is perhaps no coincidence that during this period, in Italy the term "creative" acquired a new significance, indicative of a society undergoing a significant transformation: the new connotations of "productive," "inventive," "imaginative" became common usage in Italian. The transformation of the adjective "creativo" (creative) into a noun "indicating a specific professional activity completed this semantic mutation (the term was included in the prestigious dictionary Zingarelli for the first time in 1970, defined as 'a person who creates advertising')" (Melucci 1994a, p. 11).

This semantic trajectory had its counterpart in the change that simultaneously affected those involved in creativity; generally speaking, attention shifted progressively from the genius to the "man in the street," from wide-eyed admiration for the transcendental intuitions of the former to the satisfied and instrumental recognition of the effective problem-solving strategies of the latter. In parallel, the amazement that previously accompanied that which was creative, as observed through religious imagination or aesthetic research, was gradually replaced by investigation.

An exemplary formulation of this second paradigm is offered by Margaret Boden, a well-known English researcher who specialized in cognitive sciences. She effectively describes the object of our study in these terms: "Creativity draws crucially on our ordinary abilities. Noticing, remembering, seen, speaking, hearing, understanding language and recognizing analogies: all these talents of Everyman are important. [...] [Creatives] are in a sense more free than us, for they can generate possibilities that we cannot imagine. Yet, they respect constraints *more* than we do, not less" (Boden 1990, p. 245 and p. 254).

There are several points that will require further study during the course of our investigation. First of all, creativity is a human potential, therefore "of everyone," structured in the dynamics of our species: the topic of creativity has often been confined to aesthetics, "even though the creative process is immensely important for any sort of inquiry" (Maddalena 2015, p. 85). It has to do with our ability to establish a relationship with the daily reality that surrounds us, a relationship, we might add, capable of generating the "sense" of everyday life. The philosopher Helmut Plessner surmised that "the mystery of creativity, of the brilliant idea, consists in the successful move, in the encounter between man and things" (Plessner 1928, It. trans. 2006, p. 345). In the same period, the prominent American scholar, philosopher, and educational reformer, John Dewey, came to the same conclusions in an attempt to derive strategies to enhance this precious energy. If, on the one hand, it is understandable that the creative mind be associated with rare and unique individuals (the geniuses), this must be tempered with the observation that every individual is, in his own way, "unique": each individual experiences life from a different perspective, and consequently "has something distinctive to give to others if he can transform his experiences into ideas and transmit them to others" (Dewey 1930, p. 3).

Returning to Boden, there is one final aspect incorporating some very significant developments to be emphasized: creativity has to do with the ability to generate "analogies," to create "connections," "more possibilities." This is an ability that has not been identified, at these levels, in any other living species. Creativity makes us "freer," precisely because it finds more solutions than a simple mechanical recording of data would be able to do. Yet, and this is a conclusion that heralds both theoretical and practical consequences, creativity does not coincide with fantasy of which it makes abundant use: creativity finds its peak and its *raison d'être* precisely in the "constrained" condition of our daily living.

It is a structural ability: a mandatory path tracing the roots of such extraordinary potential is written into the very structure of our being in the world. What emerges is that the more we investigate that which is taken for granted, the everyday, the mundane, the more we find ourselves inevitably (regardless of our awareness) identifying the need to leap beyond that "here and now," to exert that exclusive ability and urgency to "transcend" the space and time of our action, even the most common, distracted, and identify an unavoidable re-leap "from earth to heaven":

therefore, if creative innovation is one of the characteristics of human action, the constant openness to new possibilities "shows the dimension of transcendence inherent in individual and collective action and is directly connected to the reflexivity of self-consciousness" (Crespi 2010, p. IX).

In this conceptual framework, creativity, in all its different wavelengths, is fundamental for our survival: by using creativity "we find a lost child, [...] we procure the necessary food and make our way in a new place and in a new culture [...], whether it's about raising our child, advising a friend, arranging our house or planning a fundraising event" (Ruth 2007, p. 26).

Certainly, in recent decades the rapid processes of change that have affected the production systems sector have also contributed to upsetting classical and romantic conceptions (which, it must be remembered, have never disappeared): the idea of a good society "made up of a few geniuses capable of designing and programming the executive work of 'the great unwashed'" (De Masi 2003, p. 445) pushed scholars to focus their attention on the "peaks": with the advent of modernity, "the idea begins to prevail that every human being has a creative spark and that it needs to be nurtured for the benefit of all" (ibidem).

Recently, in an attempt to reorganize a synthetic framework of an increasingly rich and varied approach, an effort has been made to identify semantic and operational categories to "cage" an energy that is in itself constitutively uncontainable while still preserving the previous concepts. This is perhaps the root of recent theoretical efforts that have led to the creation of various frameworks and conceptualizations: the so-called model *Four-C* of creativity, for example, shows how it "can range from more subjective creative experiences (*mini-c* level of creativity) to creative processes and products recognized by others as making creative contributions in everyday (*little-c*), professional (*Pro-c*) and historical context (*Big-C*)" (van der Zandena et al. 2020, p. 2).[1]

---

[1] Recent increasingly specific and detailed studies have clarified that "whit respect to the general implications for educational practice [...] the distinction between some domains does not appear to be critically important at the little c level (i.e., everyday creativity). In other words, before the little c grows into Pro-c, which usually takes years of professional training, students' creative potential in a variety of areas should be carefully identified, valued and fulfilled in schools" (Qiana et al. 2019, p. 7).

Another useful concept is that which distinguishes whether a new idea is original in absolute terms or only in a particular context. A "creative arbitrage" has been hypothesized, drawing a comparison with the economic phenomenon of so-called financial arbitrage, which involves buying in one market and selling in another. While "generative" creativity occurs when someone comes up with a new idea, creative arbitrage occurs "when someone exports an idea from a context in which the idea is already known to a context in which it is not" (Fleming et al. 2007, p. 467).

As can be imagined, the difficulty in creating a satisfactory framework for the definition and analysis of the creative act is linked to the fact that while, on the one hand, it is recognized globally as a process, as a form of behavior, as an outcome, as a desirable ability, on the other, "the meanings, the behaviors, the outcomes are culture-specific" (Reuter 2015, p. 54).

Moreover, despite the undeniable progress made in the theoretical field, in recent decades new problems and a certain dissatisfaction at methodological "level" have come to light: in particular, the "I" paradigm ended up generating partial theoretical models that investigate human activity "in a social vacuum and conceptualize creativity as a quality of the lone individual" (Glăveanu 2010, p. 82). Hence the urgency of finding a new, further paradigm.

1.2.3 The "We" Paradigm

The objective of the "we" paradigm is to fill this theoretical and practical gap in the observation of concrete creative dynamics: in this context, creativity is considered not simply and exclusively as an expression of the individual but also, and mainly, as a result of human interaction and collaboration. Glăveanu, entering into a veiled controversy with the previous tradition of investigation, intends to propose his "social psychology of creativity" in explicit terms; while it is true that in the early 1980s the American psychologist Teresa Amabile began proposing a specific social psychology of creativity, it must be admitted that much of the work done in that sphere "still endorses a vision of the social that corresponds more to individualistic paradigms than to a truly social perspective" (Glăveanu 2010, p. 83).

Having clarified this, we can now proceed to the topics inherent to the area of our study and, with all due caution, we can agree with the statement that "sociology is the ideal domain to investigate creativity" (Reuter 2015, p. 42), especially in its two main aspects of investigation: (a) the influence exerted by the social context on creative persons and creativity and (b) creativity expressed "not by individuals but by groups" (De Masi 2003, p. 433). Sociology is becoming increasingly interested in processes by which individual genius can be, and indeed is, combined with the collective genius of organized groups.

In adopting this perspective, however, we believe an attempt must be made to trace the deep roots of the relational dimension of the creative impulse, an impulse that a number of scholars consider represents a "congenital" factor of the very structure of the human being.

1.3   Creativity and/Is Transcendence

"While the life of the animal is centric, the life of man, who cannot break the centration and at the same time is projected beyond it, is eccentric" (Plessner 1928, It. trans. 2006, p. 315). The German philosopher and sociologist Helmuth Plessner has provided us with this imaginative description of the human condition and its uniqueness in the framework of living beings: it is an attempt to metaphorically explain the strange situation in which we human beings find ourselves, forced as we are to transcend the "here and now" of everyday life. While all animals have to do is remain in the circle of their reactivity, this dynamic, although it is a condition in the development of human existence, turns out to be dramatically and confusingly insufficient: we are bound by a "centration" that we are constantly called to overcome, to question, to "transcend."

Philosophy, but also art, has repeatedly tried to focus on this point of irreducible distinction between human beings and animals. Perhaps however it is best illustrated by the Italian poet Giacomo Leopardi in his

"Night Song of a Wandering Shepherd of Asia"[2]: his shepherd ponders the strange phenomenon whereby, while his flock of sheep is contented to sit in the shade *on the grass*, even if he follows their example he cannot achieve the same tranquility. For him, sitting there does not bring serenity, there is a *"weight"* on his mind, *"a sense of weariness"* eternally robbing him of *"rest and place."*

However, this is a dynamism that tends to reach the limit, in the unmanageable need to surpass it: it is, according to the American psychologist Rollo May, that primordial move, that tendency evident in all organic and human life that fuels an imperative need to expand, stretch, develop, mature, the inclination to express and activate all the organism's capacities to the limit. The primary motivation for creativity would be precisely this tendency, "since the organism establishes new relationships with the environment in the incessant attempt to become as much completely possible itself" (May 1959, It. trans. 1972, p. 99). From this perspective, it is understandable how we can come to identify precisely in the creative impulse "the attribute that distinguishes us from other species" (Florida 2002, It. trans. 2003, p. 21), to fix its feeding source exactly in the ability to think and live beyond the simple given: our actions are always bound, but never completely determined. The fact that "we are not trapped in our perceptual here-and-now is both an indicator of creativity and of its great success" (Glăveanu 2018, p. 156).

Psychology has tried to cast this structural tendency into the concrete of everyday existence by identifying its drive even in the most elementary stimuli that characterize the human genre: the now classic "theory of basic needs" by Abraham Maslow seems to frame the universal dynamics of self-realization in the desire to become more and more what one is, "to become everything that one is capable of becoming" (see Goble 1970).

On the philosophical side, the Austrian philosopher Martin Buber indicated this primary motivation with the appropriate expression "instinct of creativity," describing it as the will to "do things." It is not simply about the pleasure of seeing a form arise from matter that was previously formless: what the child (that is, the creative being) wants is to

---

[2] From the translation by Frederick Townsend, 1887 (https://www.sas.upenn.edu/~cavitch/pdf-library/Leopardi_Poems_1887_edition.pdf).

participate in this "becoming of the thing"; he wants to be the subject of this production process. What is important is that through his own action "something is born that just a moment before, did not exist" (Buber 1926, It. trans. 1993, p. 163). The deep root of the creative instinct would therefore be sought in the ancestral desire to "participate" in the continuous flow of the incessant creation of reality.

It is not, therefore (as might be thought), a particular attitude reserved for those who develop a certain ability or intellectual, reflective, or religious inclination: on the contrary, "life, at every moment, tends to transcend the state of present things" (Jedlowski 2012, p. 3) and for this singular evidence (which is the basis of all our action and our peculiar "anxiety") "we do not know where we are going, but we are sure we must go beyond what is already given" (Melucci 1994b p. 247). And, in venturing into this uncertain enterprise, we nourish ourselves with curiosity and hope "to mobilize the individual towards the overcoming of the given, [...], towards the search for meaning" (Fabbrini 1994, p. 129).

I have hinted at the issue of "meaning" (to which I will necessarily have to return and expand). Now, here it could be established that what moves man is the drive for the search for meaning (not just philosophical or logical, but existential) of what he does: with this term we express what the Italian sociologist Franco Crespi describes as a given reality, not dependent on the subject, but an integral part of the biological and relational structure of the human being, without the possibility of definitively determining its origin. Meaning is a "direction," both confused and irreducible: "It is existence itself that, in giving itself, gives meaning: for the simple fact that something is given, it necessarily gives meaning. The giving of something causes a difference that determines a direction, a meaning" (Crespi 2005, p. 26).

Meaning, therefore, is a directionality that, however confused and uncertain, forces us to set ourselves in motion, "regardless," we might almost say: regardless of clarity, regardless of success, regardless of desire, and regardless of culture. Crespi defines it as pre-cultural. As will be seen later, Hans Joas describes this drive as inherent in the body itself, as "something the body does" at a pre-conscious level. Taking up some key concepts of Merleau-Ponty such as "pre-reflective" or "pre-predicative," the German sociologist uses them to refer to "the givenness of the world prior to all act of reflection or predication" (Joas 1996, p. 179).

This "meaning," which makes reality perceived as "also something" (Plessner 1928, It. trans. 2006, p. 313), which sets human action in motion, has as its peculiar dynamism the ability to transcend limits through its most effective weapon in this unstoppable and always imperfect enterprise: the imaginary.

Michael Polanyi defined it as the set of "all thoughts of things that are not present, or that are not yet present—perhaps never be present—acts of the imagination" (Polanyi 2009, p. 155). When we raise an arm, we give body to an intention that is an act of imagination (not visual but muscular): therefore, an athlete preparing to jump is engaged in an intense act of "muscular imagination."

Before delving into the characteristics of this extravagant human ability, however, I would follow the path set and unresolved by a marveling Émile Durkheim in front of this strange phenomenon: "Only man has the ability to conceive the ideal and add it to the real. Where does this singular privilege come from?" (Durkheim 1912, It. trans. 1973, p. 485). I will try to answer this eccentric, almost impertinent question. Where does this "singular privilege" come from?

There is an interesting psychoanalytic perspective to be considered that attempts to find the roots of creativity in an original trauma. On our arrival in the world, a trauma occurs in our unconscious life, i.e., the detachment from the maternal figure, a loss of the object of love that lies at the base of our subsequent feelings of aggression and guilt. In this dimension straddling awareness and unconsciousness, "the desire to repair guilt is expressed in the attempt to recreate the bond that has been broken" (Melucci 1994a, p. 16). Using other investigative tools, the well-known Polish composer Frédéric Chopin had reached a similar insight, similarly and metaphorically dealing with the bond of fatherhood and therefore of sonship: "The only misfortune is that we are the work of a famous luthier, of a Stradivari *sui generis*, who is no longer here to repair us. We do not know how to emit new sounds under inept hands and we choke inside; for lack of a luthier no one will know how to draw [sounds] from us anymore" (letter to Julian Fontana, August 18, 1848). Creativity, therefore, would be the expression of this "reparative instance" that faces "a very primitive and very deep experience of rupture and destruction" (Melucci 1994a, p. 16).

Freud expended much energy in attempting to unravel the mysterious knot of genius, especially the initial spring that drives creativity, concluding that fantastical worlds are created by both the child and the artist from the same motivating impulse: the desire to satisfy an unfulfilled desire (see Freud 1907/1989).

Assuming this is the "why" of the creative drive, I will try, symmetrically, to identify the "how": it is obvious that ordinary expressiveness cannot aspire to solve problems of this magnitude; it serves much simpler and instrumental dynamics and procedures. In the face of transcendental shortcomings, however, man "continually believes he needs extraordinary means for his satisfaction" (Plessner 1928, It. trans. 2006, p. 362). These "extraordinary means" (to resume the Durkheimian line of thought) coincide with the imaginative capacity, with the imaginary, with the possibility of seeing things as "also something." Hence the dizzying connection between self-realization drive and creative attitude: "Learning and creativity are essential for self-actualization" (Burleson 2005, p. 437).

Biology has also intervened with its own contribution in trying to define the operational framework of human creative energy: Edmund Sinnott, an American botanist, identifies the imagination as the most distinctive human characteristic of all, precisely because it makes creativity possible. He observes that the astonishing acceleration made on the road to progress could not be adequately explained by the human craving to achieve goals, to satisfy a scheme of desires. None of the innovations made would have been possible if there had not been someone capable of "imagining" a situation never experienced before, capable of mentally picturing something that had never seen before: "The problem of creativity is reduced, in the end, to the problem of how these new ideas originate" (Sinnott 1959, It. trans. 1972, p. 43).

I repeat: it is not just about the faculty of fantasizing, which is an expressive form typical of childhood, but about a way of looking at how certain things "connect" with others. We could hazard that in this (and probably "only" in this) man is truly a "creator": in generating connections that are only present in reality through his "symbolic" actions.

The state of lack that qualifies our being in the world (of whatever type it may be) is what drives us and forces us to use our ability to establish connections between what is here and now and what is not here but can be evoked, projecting us beyond the concrete objectivity of things: "If our substance were really given to us, and we had it at hand, we would undoubtedly not project ourselves beyond what limits us. But we are insufficient to ourselves" (Duvignaud 1967, It. trans. 1969, p. 134).

Psychology helps us again by identifying a possible demarcation point in the realm of the biological, between the animal and the being-of-culture, capable of "figuring absence." Dreaming, predicting, anticipating, projecting, inventing, overcoming of the sensible given, "certainly represent the highest expression of man's power and responsibility towards the world; they constitute the most sophisticated processes of his contact with the environment" (Fabbrini 1994, p. 128).

These are very "slippery" investigative areas for scientific research methodologies, areas where the discourse tends to become vague and mysterious, to be confined so far in the numbers of uncertain knowledge: "Biologists, like all serious scientists, have hesitated to venture into a speculative field that touches on that of metaphysics, since both enjoy today a reputation not excessively flattering in scientific circles" (Sinnott 1959, It. trans. 1972, pp. 45 and 49).

It can be agreed that this "overcoming of the sensible data" has been expressed, in the history of humanity, through forms of investigation more or less explicitly dedicated to this great enterprise, such as philosophical reflection, religious experience, and aesthetic production. We can therefore agree with Adorno, who believes that only the latter "allows men to grasp in authentic artistic configurations, the possibility that there is something more than the mere existence they lead, something more than the arrangements of the world to which they are irremediably bound" (Adorno 1956, It. trans. 1990, p. 131).

The "high" creativity, what we normally define as "artistic" (*big-C*), would therefore have the ponderous task of helping man in this immense effort to reconstruct the "ultimate" senses of existence: in this perspective, art would document the attempt to express a sense ungraspable by other forms of knowledge and representation. The peculiarity of the artistic product is therefore revealed in the fact that it would be "an objectification whose function is to show the unobjectifiable, or the proper limit of every form of determination" (Crespi 2010, p. X). This is why artists and creative scientists "transcend themselves" in a certain sense as bearers of tradition, "they have not only gone beyond it, they have gone beyond themselves; they have transcended their Selves" (Briskman 2009, p. 41).

Nevertheless, if the observations made so far hold true, we are forced to investigate also, and primarily, more routine, more daily expressiveness (*little-c*), because perhaps in those we will be able to verify the potential of the imaginary and creativity as a hallmark of properly human action, regardless of the "level" of its expressive products.

I should mention here the well-known path of critical reflexivity carried out by the Austrian sociologist Alfred Schütz, unfortunately left incomplete due to his sudden death: through his work, we are led to recognize that the ability to create connections (expression with which we have defined creativity) is at the origin of every elementary dynamic of knowledge and construction of meaning. For Schütz, the "world of life," our daily existence, is not flat, horizontal, without fractures: we should rather represent it as the result of numerous "stratifications" because "the life-world embraces still more than everyday reality [...]. Man relinquishes the everyday natural attitude in order to lapse into fictive world, into fantasies" (Schütz and Luckmann 1973, p. 21).

If therefore the daily round is made up of many "finite provinces of meaning" (i.e., "meaning-compatible experiences" p. 23), the real problem turns out to be that of being able to hold together a series of experiences that are not "naturally" connected to each other: they are, on the contrary, "provinces of reality with finite structure of meaning" that do not have an automatic ability to dialogue with each other and that instead have boundaries that cannot be crossed without resorting to "transcendent" dynamics.

The only way to reconnect what is not connected by nature is the great invention of "symbolic relations," that we are about to explore: in this perspective, creativity can therefore be considered "the ability to 'move an idea from one state to another'" (McWilliam and Dawson 2008, p. 635), whether it is instrumental, ordinary connections or, on the contrary, of high expressive level, that depth that even tries to restore and restore "the bond with the lost object of love" (Melucci 1994a, p. 17).

1.4 The Revolution of "Symbolic Combinations"

I could establish, in this framework, that the primordial creative move (that very particular way of approaching things that constitutes the insurmountable leap between the human species and all other living beings) was exactly the ability to "organically connect" the infinite and multiform details of existence: it is like saying that human creativity (unique and never repeated in other living beings) began as an urgency and strategy to overcome the "here and now." From fire to wheel, from stilt house to stone house, from hammer to satellite, man has been able to look at things "transcending" them, stepping out of the here and now to fish from the past what can be decisive for the future, whatever latitude they belong to. The reflection on experience, the ability to treasure what was previously experienced for an improvement of future existence (ability to "project"), is at the basis of creativity and is expressed as ability to discover ("invent?") links between things that in themselves (in "nature") are disconnected.

Sociological reflection should pay more attention to the insights of the Italian polymath, Vilfredo Pareto in this specific field of investigation: perhaps the very different framework of investigation makes it difficult to establish links between his thought and that of Alfred Schütz, a relationship that here we can only hypothesize based on convergences of insights and research perspectives. It is interesting to note (and here I will limit myself to this) the many consonances between what has been said so far and what the Pareto affirms in relation to the so-called instinct of combinations, which, being part of the "non-logical" actions, constitutes, in a certain way, a *trait d'union* between the "residues" (the instincts, the passions, the emotions) and the "derivations" (reasonings and behaviors through which actions are justified).

It is important to dwell on this aspect because Pareto uses it to offer an interesting perspective capable of effectively framing the roots of human creative abilities. Indeed, the definition of creativity that has been attributed to him, which today can be found on many communication agency and Human Resources websites (*Finding new links between known things*), is not expressed in so many words in his *Treatise on general sociology*. It is however significant for at least three reasons: (a) it is very effective; (b) it can be "derived" from his thoughts; (c) it attests how much the "fever of creativity" today seeks scientific foundations to justify its pervasive development in every aspect of advanced societies.

What Pareto says, interested as he is in this particular aspect of human action, is that the ability to "combine" is what brings innovation: "The contrast between the tendency to combinations, which innovates, and the tendency to the permanence of aggregates of sensations, which conserves, could put us on the way to explain many facts of human societies" (Pareto 1916, ed. 1988, p. 154). In practice, this "instinct" defines that strange disposition of man to innovate, invent, and produce new facts and links, through imagination and non-logical action: the instinct of combinations "is considered particularly strong in man, probably being at the origin of the development of human civilization" (Padua 2017, p. 11).

Whether it is a question of expressiveness, art, technology, discovery, or invention, the dynamics are always the same, the "connection of points," as Steve Jobs explained referring to his well-known creative enterprise, *Connecting Dots*. On the other hand and similarly, the discovery of previously unknown relationships is a central goal of scientific research: theoretical models like geographical maps, for example, show connections between previously unknown events. Like the geographical maps of unknown regions, "theories present white spaces to indicate connections not yet known" (Elias 1978, It. trans. 1990, p. 189).

Creativity, therefore, is based on technologies that are already available in existing institutions and a creative idea can be defined in a certain sense as "a reformulation of existing ideas" (Rogoff 1990, p. 198) or (with a very creative expression) as the set of "extraordinary products of ordinary cognitive operations combined in unordinary ways" (Dasgupta

2019, p. VIII).[3] Equally useful for its development in this investigation is the definition for which being creative means using old ideas "in a new guise called analogy" (Markman and Wood 2009). Perhaps this was the intuition on which Charles Sanders Peirce based his powerful aphorism that states if an idea is completely new it will almost certainly be stupid: creative novelty makes it possible to "propose, increase, or foster new ways of old habits or new habits, as far as we can call something 'new' (absolute novelty is impossible)" (Maddalena 2015, p. 81). For this reason, our creative gestures always "present only slight differences from contexts, habits, and gestures that precede them. Creation is never 'out of the blue'" (ibid., p. 97).

It can be said, therefore, that it is the ability (or necessity) to find new connections that plumbs the most ancestral areas of the human being, eager to find a meaning where it does not appear or does not seem possible.

In extreme synthesis, it could be affirmed that the first form of human creativity was the "*invention of sense*": "Is creativity not a perennial characteristic of every kind of sign? Sure enough, to a certain degree any semiosis is creative" (Maddalena 2015, p. 89).

This is a prerogative of our species that has developed to unthinkable levels thanks to a competence we assume is present only in the human being: the "symbolic" ability. Even if we consider the instinctive actions typical of animals as elementary forms of sense construction (which man also continues to use, among other things), the dynamics are still of a different nature and far from the simple ability to conceive that $1 + 1 = 2$ (logical-symbolic sequence attributable equally to apples, slaps, kisses, or dreams).

I must therefore pursue my investigations into this strange and revolutionary ability because man "is able to transcend everydayness by means of symbols" (Schütz and Luckmann 1973, p. 21). For the Austrian sociologist the harmony and compatibility of our real experiences are limited, as we have seen, to a "certain province of meaning." What makes this

---

[3] "But what kind of reality do we create? Of course, we are not at all speaking of creation ex nihilo. We reshape in a new way a long path of concepts, ideas, and materials. In a pragmatist way we could say that we reshape "experience" broadly understood" (Maddalena 2015, p. 93).

situation extremely awkward is the fact that it is not possible to reduce a finite province of meaning to another with the help of a "conversion formula": in practice, I cannot connect a flower to a feeling for a young lady whose glance "struck" me. There is not, that is, a kind of "genetic mutation" that can connect a flower to a woman, except through the creation of a "symbolic" connection: a bunch of flowers becomes a symbol of a feeling, transcending itself and, together, the finiteness of the provinces [flower] [woman] [emotion] [project]. The transition from one province of meaning to another "can only be accomplished by means of a 'leap' (in Kierkegaard's sense) [...]. In the course of a day, indeed of an hour, we can, through the modifications of the tension of consciousness, traverse a whole series of such provinces" (ibid., p. 24).

In support of this observation, Schütz offers a series of "daily" examples of leaps perceived as "natural," which in reality are not natural at all: cutting off a daydream to get to work, stumbling while staring at a picture, "entering the scene," starting to "play," being assailed by hunger or by any stimulus during scientific, aesthetic, religious contemplation, etc. Only when we experience a specific shock that for a moment breaks through the limits of what is "Real" for us (finite province of meaning), we must "transfer (or 'wish' to) the accent of reality to another province of meaning" (ibid., p. 25).

This inevitable dynamism, continues Schütz, leads us, in daily life, to confer "the accent of reality" to a single specific province of meaning, in such a way that the other provinces of meaning can only appear as "quasi-realities": therefore, "among the various levels of reality there is however only one that is thematic at any given time, while the others appear subordinate, 'ancillary'" (Gattamorta 2005, p. 83). For this reason, paradoxically, looking at life from a scientific or a religious perspective, "the everyday life-world can be seen as a quasi-reality" (Schütz and Luckmann 1973, p. 25).

From this point of view, the three different types of transcendences, *small, medium, large,* have in common the fact of overcoming the "here and now of the world" at hand. For the purpose of this book, it is sufficient to consider specifically the third type, in which transcendence surpasses the limits of everyday life through "symbols": the transcendences with which the symbolic significant references come to terms belong to finite provinces of meaning "that surpass the boundaries of daily reality (they are the world of scientific theory, religion, politics, art, play, but also of imagination and dream)" (Gattamorta 2005, p. 71).

I am now approaching the most promising field of application for this investigation, which provides the most suitable tools to "create connections" between realities that would not "naturally" connect. Schütz uses an interesting neologism to indicate this particular power to establish links between non-communicating elements, overcoming "finiteness" through symbolic dynamics; for him, the symbol, in fact, does not "represent," it "presents," in other words, it "makes present": transcending the limits of time and space, it is able to "bring America into the living room" simply by using linguistic sounds, letters, icons. Schütz's thesis is that representative references have the function of "overcoming the transcendences that belong to the reality of everyday life" (ibid., p. 79): through this peculiar ability (symbolization) "man tries to learn these transcendent phenomena in a way similar to our perceptible world" (Schütz 1955, It. trans. 1979, p. 300).

More precisely, the symbol is defined by Schütz as a representative reference of a higher order, in which one representing member of the pair is an object, a fact, or an event within the reality of our everyday life, while the other "refers to an idea that transcends our experience of everyday life" (ibid., p. 303).

It must be admitted that these reflections are not simple, but their relevance to the specific content of this investigation (creativity as the ability to generate connections) is highlighted by a publication with a strongly different approach that appeared a few years after these insights. Arthur Koestler's successful essay *The Act of Creation* was published in New York in 1964: in it, the Hungarian born writer, journalist, essayist, philosopher, and latterly parapsychologist identified the decisive phase of creativity as capacity "to perceive … a situation or event in two habitually incompatible associative contexts" (Koestler 1964, p. 95). He also argued, in that very successful booklet, that we reach our maximum level of creative ability "when rational thought is suspended—for example, in dreams and trance-like states. Then the mind is capable of receiving inspiration and insight" (ibid.).

As can be imagined, this juggling of the worlds of things and their meaning, but also of their concrete instrumental uses, continues to move along dreamy frontiers, with a romantic flavor.

1.5   Intelligences

Another approach to the issues addressed here, very promising for expanding the depth of the investigation, is that linked to the relatively recent and much debated interdisciplinary reflection on intelligence: some pioneering studies in the field of human sciences (especially of a psychological, psychoanalytic, sociological, and pedagogical nature) have begun to analyze their specific and multifaceted fields of application (with the related different knowledge methodologies), helping in part to overcome that incommunicability between the world of reason and calculation and that of sensations, emotions, intuitions.

I would mention here as an example of a reflection of great originality that which linked the sudden development of man's intellectual abilities, from the origin of every "significant action," with the appearance of the "opposable thumb," decisive for the structuring of the prehensile hand, enabling it to "grasp" objects: "At this point man began to produce thoughts on the nature of the object he had in hand" (Sennett 2008, It. trans. 2009, p. 149). Many residual expressions still exist in today's parlance, metaphorically indicating this revolution of reflexivity: "Having a good grip on the subject," "Grasping a problem," are nothing more than "figurative ways of speaking that reflect the evolutionary dialogue that took place between the hand and the brain" (ibid.).

In this way, the process of "learning" is brought back to its semantic (and probably evolutionary) origin of "stretching out a hand and tightening it on an object," asking for its meaning, possible usefulness. From these premises, the next (almost natural) step was to reconsider intelligence as the vast and varied human ability to face existence as a "problem to solve," as the revolutionary tool not only to respond to the "provocations" of the "centric" reality (which, as has been seen, man shares with animals) but also to try to solve more complex, transcendent, "eccentric" problems.

These considerations are at the basis of the so-called Theory of multiple intelligences of the American psychologist Howard Gardner whose fundamental thesis (subject to various objections) is that there are specific intellectual abilities for different fields and that each individual is tuned, depending on the type of prevailing intelligence, to certain cognitive possibilities rather than others: in this way it is possible to explain, paradoxically, how it can happen that "geniuses" are unable to solve "elementary" problems. The various types of intelligence, in fact (linguistic, musical, logical-mathematical, spatial, bodily kinesthetic, personal, relational) are not necessarily interconnected nor mechanically developed individually and measurable as the famous intelligence quotient (IQ).

It is important to follow these developments in research because they introduce an element that has been underestimated or left to "chance" for centuries," the dimension of the "context" in which creativity can find the fertile ground of its development. If it is true that every individual has a predisposition toward specific intellectual abilities, creativity will be the result of the encounter between their particular type of prevailing intelligence and the external conditions that facilitate its use. The context (literally erased in romantic culture unless as an occasional "prompt" for the genius) begins to be considered a k ingredient of creative expressiveness. Therefore, applying the theory of multiple intelligences to creativity leads us to recognize that it manifests "when the individual endowed with a certain type of intelligence encounters cultural and social conditions that allow him to develop that capacity to the maximum, rather than inhibit it or divert it towards other fields where it is destined to fail" (Melucci 1994a, p. 19). In this way, intelligence (and, consequently, creativity) can no longer be considered in an abstract manner, detached from the context in which they are realized and evaluated.

Two very effective anecdotes by the American psychologists Robert Sternberg and Louise Spear-Swerling render immediately comprehensible the polemical force of this approach compared to traditional unitary theories of IQ.

Two boys with vastly different IQs venture into a forest when suddenly a huge, hungry grizzly bear appears and stares at them: the first boy (the one who performs better academically) calculates that the grizzly will reach them in exactly 17.3 s and panics. Frozen with terror, he looks at the second boy who, with absolute calm, "takes off his hiking boots and puts on his jogging shoes. The first boy says to the second: You're crazy. It's impossible to run faster than that grizzly! The second boy replies: That's true. But I just need to run faster than you!" (Sternberg and Spear-Swerling 1996, It. trans. 2002, p. 17).

In the second episode reported by the two authors, young Jack considers Irvin to be the dumbest in the class, so he likes to tease him and publicly demonstrate his inferiority. Together with a friend, he offers Irvin two coins, a nickel and a *dime*, telling him he can choose which of the two he wants. Irvin chooses the larger one, the nickel, and leaves. An adult who was watching the exchange from afar approaches Irvin and kindly explains that the *dime* is worth more than the nickel, even though it's smaller, and therefore he lost five *cents*. "Oh, I know, 'Irvin replies,' but if I had taken the dime, Jack would no longer have asked me to choose between the two coins; this way he will continue to ask me. I've already taken more than a dollar from him, and all I have to do is choose the nickel" (ibid., p. 13).

The transition from "multiple intelligence" to "multiple creativity" is in a sense automatic: "Gardner applied the theory of multiple intelligences to understand creativity. He suggested that great creative minds often have relied on different intelligences to manifest their creativity" (Sternberg 2005, p. 374).

Now to draw the conclusions of this first chapter of investigation: the connection between the concept of "intelligences" and creativity allows us to hypothesize a broader framework, in which the different "powers" of the human mind can proceed independently, but (an aspect extraordinarily rich in cognitive consequences) can also "influence" each other in diverse ways: "Creativity is multidimensional and manifests itself in many forms, each of which strengthens the other" (Florida 2002, It. trans. 2003, p. 24). The dialogue between these multifaceted potentials is perhaps one of the most promising fields of investigation and experimentation of our times: the various forms of creativity that we normally consider different from each other (technology, economy, arts) are potentially correlated since they not only use similar mental processes, "but they reinforce each other through processes of cross-fertilization and the exchange of stimuli" (ibid., p. 58).

As with any respectable theory of human science, of course, also in this case "some theorists reject the idea of multiple-domain creativities" (Sternberg 2005, p. 374) and "the question of whether creativity is domain specific or domain general still remains one of the main unresolved issues in the field of creativity" (Qiana et al. 2019, p. 2). Due to this state of affairs, "perhaps the most popular position today is that creativity has both domain-specific and domain-general aspects" (Sternberg 2005, p. 375).

However that may be, there is in any case the necessity and usefulness of "contextualizing" these processes, removing them from the frequent and ineffective "scholastic" reductionism through a shift in attention toward the cultural and relational conditions "that allow or hinder the maximum possibility of expansion of the individual's creative abilities" (Melucci 1994a, p. 21).

References

Adorno T.W. (1956), *Dissonanzen. Musik in der verwalteten Welt,* Göttingen, It. trans. *Dissonanze,* Feltrinelli, Milano, 1990.

Anderson H.H. (1959), *Preface,* in Anderson H.H. (ed.), Creativity and its Cultivation, Harper & Row, New York, It. trans. *La creatività e le sue prospettive,* La scuola, Brescia 1972.

Batey M., Furnham A., Safiullina X. (2010), *Intelligence, general knowledge and personality as predictors of creativity,* in "Learning and Individual Differences", 20: 532-535.

Bauman Z. (2012), *Conversazioni sull'educazione,* Erickson, Trento.

Boden M. (1990), *The creative mind: myths and mechanism,* Basic Books, New York.

Briskman L. (2009), *Creative Product and Creative Process in Science and Art,* in Krausz M., Dutton D., Bardsley K. (ed.), *The Idea of Creativity,* Brill, Leiden-Boston.

Buber M. (1926), *Rede über das Erzieherische,* Lambert Schneider, Heilderberg, It. trans. *Il principio dialogico e altri saggi,* Edizioni San Paolo, Milano, 1993.

Burleson W. (2005), *Developing creativity, motivation, and self-actualization with learning systems,* in "Int. J. Human-Computer Studies", 63: 436–451.

Crespi F. (2005), *Sociologia del linguaggio,* Laterza, Roma-Bari.

Crespi F. (2010), *Prefazione*, in Savonardo L., *Sociologia della musica. La costruzione sociale del suono dalle tribù al digitale*, Utet, Torino.

Dasgupta S. (2019), *A Cognitive Historical Approach to Creativity*, Routledge, London – New York.

De Masi D. (2003), *La fantasia e la concretezza*, Milano, Rizzoli.

Dewey J. (1930), *Construction and Criticism*, New York: Columbia University Press.

Durkheim É. (1912), *Les formes élémentaires de la vie religieuse*, Alcan, Paris, It. trans. *Le forme elementari della vita religiosa e il sistema totemico in Australia*, Meltemi, Roma, 2005.

Duvignaud J. (1967), *Sociologie de l'art*, Presses Universitaires de France, Paris; It. trans. *Sociologia dell'arte*, Il Mulino, Bologna 1969.

Elias N. (1978), *Was ist Soziologie?*, München, Juventa, It. trans. *Che cos'è la sociologia?*, Torino, Rosemberg & Sellier, 1990.

Fabbrini A. (1994), *Ri-creare il mondo. Adolescenti e creatività*, in Melucci A. (ed.), *Creatività: miti, discorsi, processi*, Feltrinelli, Milano.

Federici R. (2006), *Elementi sociologici della creatività. La centralità creativa degli autori del pensiero classico*, FrancoAngeli, Milano.

Finney Botti H. (1994), *La creatività nel mondo delle organizzazioni*, in Melucci A. (ed.), *Creatività: miti, discorsi, processi*, Feltrinelli, Milano.

Fleming L., Mingo S., & Chen D. (2007), *Collaborative Brokerage, Generative Creativity, and Creative Success*, in "Administrative Science Quarterly", 52: 443-475.

Florida R. (2002), *The rise of the creative class*, Basic Books, New York, It. trans. *L'ascesa della nuova classe creativa*, Mondadori, Milano, 2003.

Freud S. (1907/1989), *Creative writers and day-dreaming*, in P. Gay (Ed.), *The Freud reader* (pp. 436–443), New York: Norton.

Gattamorta L. (2005), *Teorie del simbolo. Studio sulla sociologia fenomenologica*, Milano, FrancoAngeli.

Glăveanu V.P. (2010), *Paradigms in the study of creativity: Introducing the perspective of cultural psychology*, in "New Ideas in Psychology", 28: 79-93.

Glăveanu V.P. (2018), *Educating which creativity?*, in "Thinking Skills and Creativity", 27: 25-32.

Goble F. (1970), *The Third Force: The Psychology of Abraham Maslow A Revolutionary New View of Man*, Pocket Books, New York, NY.

Guilford, J. P. (1950), *Creativity*, in "American Psychologist", 5: 444-454.

Hernández-Torrano D., Ibrayeva L. (2020), *Creativity and education: A bibliometric mapping of the research literature (1975–2019)*, in "Thinking Skills and Creativity" 35, 100625.

Jaussi K.S., Dionne S.D. (2003), *Leading for creativity: The role of unconventional leader behaviour,* in "The Leadership Quarterly", 14: 475-498.

Jedlowski P. (2012), *Il senso del futuro. I quadri sociali della capacità di aspirare,* in de Leonardis O., Deriu M. (ed.), *Il futuro nel quotidiano. Studi sociologici sulla capacità di aspirare,* Egea, Milano.

Joas H. (1996), *The creativity of action,* Chicago, The University of Chicago press.

Koestler A. (1964), *The Act of Creation,* Penguin Books, New York.

Lindqvist G. (2003), *Vygotsky's Theory of Creativity,* in "Creativity Research Journal", 15(2&3): 245-251.

Maddalena G. (2015), *The Philosophy of Gesture. Completing Pragmatists' Incomplete revolution,* McGill-Queen's University Press, Montreal & Kingston, London, Chicago.

Markman A., Wood K. (2009), *The Cognitive Science of Innovation Tools,* in Markman A., Wood K. (Eds), *Tools for Innovation,* Oxford England: Oxford University Press.

May R. (1959), *The nature of creativity,* in Anderson H.H. (ed.), *Creativity and its Cultivation,* Harper & Row, New York, It. trans. *La creatività e le sue prospettive,* La scuola, Brescia 1972.

McWilliam E., Dawson S. (2008), *Teaching for creativity: towards sustainable and replicable pedagogical practice,* in "High Education" 56: 633-643.

Meheus J., Nickles T. (1999. 2000), *The Methodological Study of Creativity and Discovery – Some Background,* in "Fonduations of Science", 4: 231-235.

Melucci A. (1994a), *Creatività: miti, discorsi, processi,* in Melucci A. (ed.), *Creatività: miti, discorsi, processi,* Feltrinelli, Milano.

Melucci A. (1994b), *L'esperienza della creatività,* in Melucci A. (ed.), *Creatività: miti, discorsi, processi,* Feltrinelli, Milano.

Nakamura J., Csikszentmihalyi M. (2003), *Creativity in Later Life,* in SAWYER R.K., et al., *Creativity and development,* Oxford University Press, New York, 186-216.

Padua D. (2017), *L'azione non-logica paretiana,* in Padua D. (ed.) *La sociologia tra modernità e postmodernità,* Morlacchi Editore, Perugia.

Pareto V. (1916), *Trattato di sociologia generale,* Barbera, Firenze, riedizione 1988 Utet, Torino.

Plessner H. (1928), *Die Stufen des Organischen und der Mensch; Einleitung in die philosophische Anthropologie,* W. de Gruyter, Berlin; It. trans. *I gradi dell'organico e l'uomo: introduzione all'antropologia filosofica,* Bollati Boringhieri, Torino, 2006.

Polanyi M. (2009), *The Creative Imagination,* in Krausz M., Dutton D., Bardsley K. (ed.), *The Idea of Creativity,* Brill, Leiden-Boston.

Qiana M., Pluckerb J.A., Yangc X. (2019), *Is creativity domain specific or domain general? Evidence from multilevel explanatory item response theory models*, in "Thinking Skills and Creativity", 33: 100571.

Reuter M.E. (2015), *Creativity – A Sociological Approach*, Palgrave, London.

Richards R. (2007), (Ed.) *Everyday Creativity and New Views of Human Nature. Psychological, Social and Spiritual Perspectives*, Washington, D.C.: American Psychological Association. Greenwich, Connecticut: Ablex Publishing Corporation.

Rogoff B. (1990), *Apprenticeship in thinking: Cognitive development in social context*, New York: Oxford University Press.

Ruth R. (2007), *Everyday Creativity: Our Hidden Potential*, in Ruth R. (edited by) *Everyday Creativity and New Views of Human Nature*, Washington, DC: American Psychological Association, 25-54.

Sawyer R.K. (2003), *Emergence in Creativity and Development*, in Sawyer R.K., et al., *Creativity and development*, Oxford University Press, New York, pp. 12-60.

Schepers P., van der Berg P.T. (2007), *Social Factors of Work-Environment Creativity*, in "Journal of Business and Psychology", 21(3).

Schütz A. (1955), *Symbol, Reality and Society*, in L. Bryson, L. Finkelstein, H. Hoagland, R.M. MacIver (ed.), *Symbols and Society*, Fourteenth Symposium on Science, Philosophy, and Religion, Harper, New York, pp. 135-202; It. trans. *Simbolo, realtà e società*, in *Saggi sociologici*, ed. A. Izzo, Utet, Torino, 1979: 260-328.

Schütz A. and Luckmann T. (1973), *The Structures of Life-Word*, Evanston, Illinois, Northwestern University Press.

Sennett, R. (2008), *The craftsman*, Yale University Press, New Haven, London; It. trans. *L'uomo artigiano*, Feltrinelli, Milano 2009.

Shalley C.E., Gilson L.L. (2004), *What leaders need to know: A review of social and contextual factors that can foster or hinder creativity*, in "The Leadership Quarterly", 15: 33-53.

Sinnott E.W. (1959), *The creativity of life*, in Anderson H.H. (ed.), *Creativity and its Cultivation*, Harper & Row, New York, It. trans. *La creatività e le sue prospettive*, La scuola, Brescia 1972.

Sternberg R.J. (2005), *Creativity or creativities?*, in "Int. J. Human-Computer Studies", 63: 370-382.

Sternberg R.J., Spear-Swerling, L. (1996), *Teaching for Thinking*, American Psychological Association, Washington, D.C.; It. trans. *Le tre intelligenze*.

Come potenziare le capacità analitiche, creative e pratiche, Erickson, Trento 2002.

van der Zandena P.J.A.C., Meijera P.C., Beghetto R.A. (2020), *A review study about creativity in adolescence: Where is the social context?,* in "Thinking Skills and Creativity", 38: 100702

2

Creativity and Contexts

Abstract In Chap. 1 I briefly traced (i) the roots and reasons for today's renewed interest in the creative faculty; (ii) the cultural and psycho-social paradigms with which it has been framed within the human sciences; (iii) the "transcendent" and "symbolic" nature of its enormous innovative capacity; and, finally, (iv) the natural ease with which it is capable of transcending the limits of human intelligences, offering a great opportunity of empowerment.

The objective of this chapter, more markedly sociological, is to show how at the origin of creative faculty and, equally, of all its subsequent developments lies not just the capacity (more or less ingenious) of individuals but rather an active, constant, and necessary interaction between the latter and the socio-cultural context in which they operate. In other words, from here on we want to study creativity as an "emergent effect," as a phenomenon resulting from the interaction of two or more elements in the field. We will see how the social context in which it operates is not just a "wrapping": it not only borrows from the outside the tools and operational materials through which subjectivity can express itself but also proceeds (not always consciously) to construct subjectivity itself from within through the repetition of social practices. Even "motivation," perhaps the most subjective element and certainly that which is most

© The Author(s) 2024
P. P. Bellini, *The Creative Gesture*, Palgrave Studies in Creativity and Culture,
https://doi.org/10.1007/978-3-031-54219-0_2

responsible for the activation of creative practices, must therefore be read in a relational key.

Keywords Creativity and environment • Internal group • Creativity evaluation • Relationality • Socialization • Motivation • Leadership

2.1   The Social Components of the Creative Approach

Between 1957 and 1958, several important interdisciplinary symposiums were held at Michigan State University, leading to the successful publication of *Creativity and Its Cultivation* in 1959: psychologists, psychoanalysts, anthropologists, educators, and communication experts tried to take stock of the situation of studies on the subject, not sparing each other very diverse or even opposing perspectives.

I will use a point of divergence to clarify the perspective of our investigation.

In her speech, Margaret Mead explained her concept of creativity, describing it as the process that takes place in the individual, "who can be said to have performed a creative act if he does, invents, thinks something that is new to him" (Mead 1959, It. trans. 1972, p. 270). First of all, we underline the fact that the characteristic of "novelty" is a fundamental element for all the definitions we have encountered in our study of the subject: there is no creativity if something new does not happen. There is a general consensus on this: while it is true that an important part of the creative process lies in the internalization of the language and symbols of the specific production field, all this laborious acquisition is not enough to achieve a creative result. It is only a prerequisite, since "creativity results when the individual somehow combines these internalized elements and generates some new configuration" (Sawyer 2003, p. 46).

Instead, the more critical point is the apodictic (or at least obscure) statement, "new to him": if, on the one hand, in this way the emphasis (sacrosanct) is placed on the fact that novelty must be evaluated by the person who has the (creative) experience firsthand, it becomes difficult to say that the very possibility of having an experience and judging it can mature in solitude. Mead, aware of the centrality of the problem, does not back down, indeed, she raises the stakes: the young student who rediscovers in the twentieth century that in a right-angled triangle the square of hypotenuse is equal to the sum of the squares of the other two sides performs a creative act as much as Pythagoras did, "even though the implications of the discovery are zero for the cultural tradition, since the proposition stated is already part of geometry" (Mead 1959, It. trans. 1972, p. 270).

I am convinced that the subjective (even "solitary") component of the creative act is a very important aspect and should be pursued. From this point of view, we believe it is legitimate for the agent, especially if young, to defend, preserve, nourish the awareness of his irreducibility to any form of social invasiveness that inevitably results in an impoverishment of self-awareness and expressiveness of his person. Especially in an era of *crowded solitude*, or "crowded loneliness," as Bauman brilliantly coined it, the creative potential of young people is severely clouded by the pervasive obsession with "being connected" and, once you go online, "you no longer have any chance of being completely and truly alone. And if you are never alone, it will be much less likely that you will read a book for the pleasure of doing so, that you will make a drawing, that you will look out of the window imagining worlds different from your own" (Bauman 2012, p. 113).

Having said and shared *in toto* this last intimacy of the creative experience, however, it is important to consider the fact that defense of the subject's irreducibility is only one of the factors necessary for the possibility of expressing it. To return to Mead's example to clarify this observation: if Pythagoras made that leap more than two millennia ago, he did so by climbing onto the mathematics (and the mathematicians) preceding or contemporary to him. In this way he was able to evaluate the novelty of his intuition: evaluation is therefore a decisive element (as we will see) and requires clear criteria with which it can be realized.

An important aspect is the association of the American anthropologist between creativity and naivety, or infantile condition: the child (from a certain point of view, as we will clarify) is the most creative of humans and the most important challenge is how to preserve this sharp weapon of knowledge, resisting the opposite current of progressive sclerosis.

However, in that same symposium at Michigan State University, Henry Murray, a psychologist, provided a similar but richer definition. For Murray, creativity is the "occurrence of a new and at the same time valid composition" (Murray 1959, It. trans. 1972, p. 128). The addition of this simple adjective, "valid," opens up more challenging horizons. As the author himself clarifies, while the attribute "new" implies that the creative production must be characterized by innovative and original ideas, the attribute "valid" instead implies a shared evaluation among a number of people, "capable of generating valid compositions in the future (whether they generate them or not, it remains valid in itself)" (ibid.). This appearance of the *Alter* in creative dynamics is the original intuition that underlies more recent research, urging the scientific community to "reflect upon, study, and cultivate creativity as a sociocultural phenomenon" (Glăveanu et al. 2019, p. 741), because creativity is, in itself, a social fact. From this point of view, it is important to overcome easy and sterile reductions that oppose *agency* and structure: "Neither the individual nor society can exist without the other, and neither is possible without creativity" (Reuter 2015, p. 16).

Accepting this invitation would allow us to evaluate the different perspectives of investigation involved, correcting their easy radicalisms: rather than adopting holistic sociological perspectives (creativity derives from the structure) or radical psychological perspectives (creativity derives from individual genius), some researchers opt for a vision of critical realism, maintaining that it is more realistic to affirm "that some people are more creative than others and that the personal characteristics interact with situations" (Fleming et al. 2007, p. 466).

I shall therefore try to follow the path of progressive expansion of interpersonal relationships implicated in the creative experience, starting from a "subjective" perspective and moving to an "inter-subjective" perspective, trying to identify if it is possible to free this exhilarating personal expressiveness from the short circuits of illusory solipsism as well as from an ultimately mortifying instrumentality.

A narrative review that appeared recently on the journal *Thinking Skills and Creativity* helps to draw up a sort of "index" of social themes recently examined in greater depth during research on creativity: the purpose of this review was to carry out a systematic study of the factors associated with the improvement or inhibition of adolescent creativity in a sample of 65 recently published studies on authoritative international scientific journals. For convenience of exposition, the factors that help, or on the contrary, hinder the development of creative abilities are classified into four categories: individual, parental, educational, and social contextual. Among the individual factors that support the development of adolescent creativity are cited openness to experience, intrinsic motivation, while anxiety is considered the main inhibiting factor. Positive family factors include parental support and autonomous motivation along with maternal involvement. Among the educational factors supporting the development of adolescent creativity, we find the ability to balance freedom and guidance, to propose flexible and open activities, to support and encourage the ideas of the students, to ensure an atmosphere of trust and respect. Finally, the supportive social contextual factors include "providing interactions that encourage expression or challenging of ideas; and encouraging adolescents to view issues from multiple global and temporal perspectives" (van der Zandena et al. 2020, p. 1).

This framework (that drills down into various subcategories) helps us to "see" a condition from above that is often overlooked when we attempt to analyze the countless forms of human action: even in the most intimate, subjective, and creative expressive action, "the environment is not only around us, but is an intrinsic part of ourselves" (Morin 1990, p. 49).

As argued so far, the confrontation of the problem of autopoiesis or heteropoiesis in creativity must necessarily be posed, without any thought of having a formula that resolves the complex relationship: it is right, therefore, to question whether the creative process is more determined by the mind of the creator or by the context in which that mind was formed and exists, and it is plausible to conclude that "the context in which a creative group operates can facilitate its creativity or can hinder it but cannot determine it" (De Masi 2003, p. 502). Similarly, the dialectic between creative-innovative action and society (with its socially shared norms) leads back to the relationship between ideas and structures: Georg Simmel speaks of a mutual influence between the two dimensions, emphasizing the fact that ideas have a creative dimension and cannot be reduced to pure reflections of social conditions, "which, however, can affect the possibility or not of asserting the same ideas" (Savonardo 2010, p. XV).

2.1.1 Creativity and Environment

To adequately address a human resource such as creativity, a fundamental and frequently overlooked condition must be taken into consideration: "Creative outcomes cannot and do not occur in a vacuum" (Shalley and Gilson 2004, p. 35). This simple statement appears obvious, but it is more complex than it seems and we ignore it at our peril.

Two general premises regarding this study.

1. It is useful to briefly report a "logical priority" regarding the succession of events that underlie creative production. Defining a "person" as creative or defining a "process" as creative is a "second" procedure as such attribution is obviously made possible only by a previous evaluation of the "product" as creative. Therefore, a product is not creative because it was produced by a creative person or process: both are considered creative because they manage to create a product considered creative. It is the creativity of the product that has, in a sense, logical priority. Therefore, we must agree with the statement that "the creativity of the product resides not in its psychological origins, but in its objective relations to other, previous, products" (Briskman 2009, p. 25).
2. The creative product can usefully be defined as an "artifact," which, in Dasgupta's valuable reflection, must be considered a "non-natural" thing: "No artifact, no creativity" (Dasgupta 2019, p. 15). The following analysis of the characteristics of the creative artifact is very effective, establishing that it (a) is conceived or produced by a conscious being in response to some desire, need, wish, or goal; (b) is in the public domain; (c) has a structure, function, and behavior that "can be understood if and only if one take into account the artificer's need, want or goal" (ibid., p. 19). As can be imagined this choice of field also has important consequences on the object of study: the artifact

must necessarily be distinguished from the "natural" (animals, plants, landscapes, and even "machines"), since natural things "have no purpose." Hence the decisive distinction between the term "function" and the term "purpose." Based on this, it is possible, legitimate, and often also useful and necessary to identify and describe the possible functions of natural objects (plants, animals, minerals, planets, black holes, atoms, molecules) by stating that the function of the heart is to pump blood through the body: but, "to assign function is not to ascribe purpose, for purpose originates in the artificer's mind as the precondition of creation" (ibid., p. 25).

As can be imagined, combining these two general premises renders the frame of reference more complex, and at the same time paradoxically begins to clarify it. The "objective relations" of the creative object (see Briskman) go far beyond the number (albeit vast) of similar previous creative objects: it is in relation with a multitude of other factors, including its author, the relations of its author, production systems, cultural frames, economic and normative processes, social and natural events, etc. So we will start, in this tangle of relations, from the most elementary, structural, physical-biological, and then move on to the more properly socio-cultural.

I shall start, therefore, from the reflection that (as previously cited) comes from the "natural" perspective, from botany that reminds us that, even at the level of biological differentiation, there is a very evident link between evolution and context and that much of the variety of all organic life is linked to environmental variety. Hereditary factors do not rigidly determine the characteristics of the body, function, or behavior: they rather provide the tools through which the subject generates a particular response to a particular environment. Therefore, a given genetic constitution does not determine a specific quality or ability, but rather determines, "a whole repertoire of reactions to a wide range of possible environmental stimuli. The norm or the goal can be different in each environment" (Sinnott 1959, It. trans. 1972, p. 39). In summary, most of the genetic heritage does not determine characteristics but "potential to respond to the environment based on how it presents itself" (Arbiser 2004, p. 10).

These observations become even more interesting when, moving out of the biological, genetic, and also behaviorist fields, we come to deduce that, from a psychological point of view, our characteristics depend on experience, events, and social structures in which we participate and that even imagination (which we have discussed earlier) is strongly and inevitably subjected to the same process of stimuli, influences, and external constraints. Even our "aspirations" (Appadurai 2004) cannot escape this origin and this "social" destiny.

It is only from a wide-ranging investigative horizon that it will be possible to begin to shed light on phenomena that are still difficult to explain today outside of a perspective capable of integrating the different levels involved: how can we explain the historical occurrence of large concentrations of genius in certain moments in time and precise locations? A careful historian of civilizations cannot miss the singular fact that the five millennia from the seventh to the third before Christ and especially the millennium between 3500 and 2500 BC "deserve to be included among these few, large, mysterious concentrations of creativity that have occurred in the course of human history" (De Masi 2003, p. 89).

Consequently, in recent decades the need has emerged to study creative dynamics within the context in which they are activated: hence, while much research has been done on the characteristics of creative personality, there is on the contrary "an increasing need for a greater understanding of the contextual factors that may enhance or discourage creativity" (Shalley and Gilson 2004, p. 34).

In summary, we have discovered that creative production is a complex phenomenon "influenced by multiple individual-level variables as well as contextual and environmental variables" (Reiter-Palmon and Illies 2004, p. 56), giving rise to a series of insights (also of an empirical and demonstrative nature) aimed at identifying more precisely "the different individual and experiential variables that have to do with individual adaptation to the social context" (Mouchiroud and Bernoussi 2008, p. 378).

More convincingly than the theory of the "genius," this perspective explains why the emergence of people with extraordinary creative capabilities is also and above all linked to dynamics intrinsically beyond the circle of their exceptional abilities. The "accessibility" factor to any expressive field is essential for creativity and represents an environmental constraint: a person cannot be creative in the abstract, but only within the rules of some practice or system of ideas. Because of this environmental constraint (among other very obvious things), "it is impossible for a child living in an isolated tribe or in an urban ghetto to become a creative mathematician, or for an athletic young to become a creative basketball player if that game is unknown in his culture" (Nakamura and Csikszentmihalyi 2003, p. 193).

For some time, the sociology of culture and communication has adopted the concept of *gatekeeper*, recognizing its central function in any learning or expressive opportunity process: it is a fundamental principle of the well-known communicative theory *Two steps flow* taken up by social psychologist Kurt Lewin who in 1952 had identified a category of individuals who connect interpersonal communication networks to the "outside," defining them as "gatekeepers." The gatekeeper controls an information flow channel so as to hold "the power to decide whether what is passing through the channel should enter or not into the group" (Katz and Lazarsfeld 1955, p. 89). Paraphrasing: Dante, Michelangelo, Mozart found themselves in the right group. It is strange to use these categories in the context of a scientific investigation: however, it must be simply and sadly admitted that "luck is an essential factor." Being in the right place at the right time makes a huge difference because objectively it is not enough to have innate talent: "One must also have access to the necessary social and cultural capital" (Nakamura and Csikszentmihalyi 2003, p. 189).[1]

To conclude and at the same time open a paragraph for further investigation, I should observe that the group of whom I am talking does not remain "on the threshold," but comes to define our most intimate perception, our "feeling" of things.

---

[1] From here, a theoretical systematization of the development of creativity has been based on the interaction of three variables: "The first is the person, who is predisposed by genetic endowment and early experience to be become in a particular realm of art or science. The second is the domain, which is the set of rules and procedures that constitute the realm in question. Finally, the third component is the field, which consists of the gatekeepers to the domain and either encourages or rejects the person's innovations to the domain" (Nakamura and Csikszentmihalyi 2003, p. 187).

2.1.2   The "Internal Group"

Every environment we "inhabit" presents different dimensions, creatively manageable to various degrees: in addition to those we could define as "natural" (linked to biological processes) and "structural" (linked to the material constraints that concrete reality imposes on experience) we also have to deal with the "social" dimensions of our daily existence. As far as our investigation is concerned, it is useful to observe (in this third perspective) that creative ability not only seems to have an individual dimension but also "seems to be above all a community value" (Federici 2006, p. 15).

The concept of the "community" dimension of creativity has been a rather recent achievement (from a theoretical point of view): when we talk about creativity we usually refer to the individual because "it is the only dimension that studies have taken into consideration" (Melucci 1994, p. 24). According to the author, this "reductionism" is the consequence of two historical-cultural reasons: the first is linked to the fact that the available research on the subject is mostly of a psychological nature (largely subjectivist); the second, already discussed, is that linked to the millennial tradition that culminates in romanticism, for which the creative dimension must be associated exclusively with extraordinary experience, with genius. On the contrary, an investigation into the links between the creative process and the social context forces us not only to abandon the romantic myth of the isolated and cursed genius "but also to question the idea of an 'I' independent from the 'things' it encounters" (Neresini 1994, p. 191).

Proceeding in this direction, the various human sciences have attempted to re-dimension the idea of creativity as an experience that takes place in solitude by highlighting the amount of social relationships necessary to make any innovative production and its evaluation possible, but even going so far as to trace the "social" roots of consciousness itself and the creative drive of the individual, including the "genius." A new awareness of identity processes, especially in the psychological and psychoanalytic fields, has come to the aid of this bold methodological and disciplinary counteroffensive: the concept of the "internal group" as presented is also very interesting, especially for its applications and its possible developments within specifically sociological research.

I will try to summarize the content of this concept: taking inspiration from various statements contained in the work of Phicon-Rivière (Argentinian psychiatrist), the concept of "internal group" comes to life from a broad reformulation of psychoanalytic theory. It is significant, for the purposes of its application in a broader field of human sciences, the fact that the idea of an internal group recognizes its most immediate ancestor in the contributions of George Herbert Mead and the Sociological School of Chicago, "thinkers to whom a decisive influence in overcoming the ancient individual-society dilemma (Tarde and Durkheim)" (Arbiser 2004, p. 10).

Ultimately, this theory asserts that individual consciousness must be considered a result of the encounter between biological disposition and socio-cultural imprint mediated through the main human groups. These structures are incorporated during evolutionary development and reproduce the social and cultural world in the individual's inner world. From this perspective, society, often considered a mere sum of individuals, becomes instead a promising research entity with which to clarify the processes through which human beings become individuals through the multifaceted unfolding of the concrete social relations in which they participate. Metaphorically, just as air, invisible and odor-free, makes the environment vital and livable for us, in the same way we float "in a semantic universe of values and contents of culture and social organization" (ibid., pp. 7 and 14). It is for this reason that gestures are "never a subjectivistic or solipsistic performance: […] there is never a solitary gesture. The gesture is always within a story" (Maddalena 2021, p. 60).

Even the most intimate human expressiveness will be the result ("emergence") of an active social relationality: the important concept of "latency" is used to indicate this original dynamic. Latency is an "exclusively human" phenomenon, considered responsible for the gap that separates us even from the other primates, our biological relatives: thanks to it, millennia of human cultural experience are assimilated in the course of a few years by each generation "latency has a central role in this process, even if not exclusive" (ibid., p. 18).

In other words, everything that has introduced us into the world indicating the meaning of *progress* remains in the depths of our being, at the origin of every action we take, at the basis of the human *agency*, even its most personal and creative aspects, so constituting the humus which nurtures it: every great innovation, therefore (in any expressive or research field), is made possible by a previous, necessary accumulation of facts and ideas.

As can be easily imagined, all this is far from leading to the easy syllogism of a social determinism that would eliminate any possibility of an original move by the individual: on the contrary, "the infinite variety of personal stories determines the singularity with which each subject decodes and processes the social universe and the cultural heritage" (ibid., p. 1). The accumulation of facts and ideas does not proceed by its own energy: when the process is at the right point, someone manages to grasp its synthesis and to arrive at the discovery "simply because on him converge the favorable cultural circumstances" (De Masi 2003, p. 519).

Recent psychology has significantly contributed to highlighting the close link existing between creativity and culture: the former uses the signs and tools provided by the latter, thus producing new cultural resources. Culture is neither external to the person nor static, but constitutive of the mind and society "offering the symbolic resources required to perceive, think, remember, imagine and, ultimately, create" (Glăveanu et al. 2019, p. 742).

Referring to the thought of the Hungarian psychologist Mihalyi Csikszentmihalyi, some scholars have recently begun to argue that it is the community, not the individual, that represents the unit of appropriate analysis in any research on how creativity is nourished. The creative process is complex because it includes the salient elements of the context with which men interact: "It is at the intersection of these interactions that the creative enterprise emerges" (McWilliam and Dawson 2008, p. 637). Where the boundary line between the two elements in play lies is not a secondary problem and not even simple to solve: it is therefore not without risks of radicalism to assert that "the true historical subject of creation is not man but society: the creative society" (De Masi 2003, p. 21).

2.1.3 Evaluation

I will now return to a theme just mentioned in passing at the beginning of this chapter: to consider an action or a production creative, it is necessary to first agree on the criteria for such evaluation. A first essential characteristic has already established: novelty. "An idea that is not novel, unusual or unique is not creative" (Hernández-Torrano and Ibrayeva 2020, p. 2). I have also observed, however, that it is necessary to decide how many other variables to involve in evaluating this novelty ("new for oneself" vs. "valid for one or more people"). I will now continue on this path of clarifications and conditions.

The political scientist Harold Lasswell also participated at the American symposia of the 1950s mentioned earlier; he was known mainly for his work on persuasive communication and on political propaganda: the basic concept from which he started his contribution at the conference was that "creativity is the disposition to make and recognize appreciable innovations" (Lasswell 1959, It. trans. 1972, p. 247). There are, in this synthetic definition, two words that we could consider "symptomatic" of a position different from the previous ones.

First of all, the dimension (disposition or intention) of "recognizability" is here intrinsically linked to creativity; second, a creative production must be able to offer a shared "appreciability" of its claim. As can be guessed, both characteristics presuppose the centrality of social interactions in order to recognize the gesture as "creative" through an interpersonal evaluation: judgments on creativity are historically situated and "there is no 'view from nowhere,' an absolute statement about what is or is not creative" (Glăveanu 2010, p. 90).

Lasswell makes his point of view explicit by stating that to identify an achievement as creative it is necessary that two complicated processes occur: the first (already reiterated), related to its innovation, must bring with it the second, "that is, a certain degree of recognition of the value of innovation" (Lasswell 1959, It. trans. 1972, p. 250). A creative work must certainly be new: yet, as many observe, novelty is not enough, because a new idea can be ridiculous or meaningless. Dreams, for example, can be new but rarely have a lasting impact on the real world. In addition to novelty, "to be creative an idea must be appropriate, recognized as socially valuable in some way for some community" (Sawyer 2003, p. 20).

In other words, if it is true, as we have said, that creative results cannot happen in a vacuum, it is equally important "to understand that ideas are not evaluated in a vacuum. When an idea is evaluated, some sort of a yardstick to which the idea is compared is necessary" (Reiter-Palmon and Illies 2004, p. 69). The two processes identified by Lasswell (innovation and recognition) only occur through the interaction between two social roles: the "innovator" (the creative) who, to be recognized as such, needs the intervention of the second protagonist, the "recognizer." Often the two individuals are already in contact with each other, sharing similar situations regarding conditions in the social context or personality type. The fact of belonging to the same civilization, the same social class, having the same interests certainly makes the operation of recognition easier. But if you intend to broaden the field, then things become more complex: the general public (and here comes the specific interest of Lasswell for mass dynamics) does not share all these aspects with the innovator and needs "the mediation of someone who is not the innovator, to pay attention to novelty" (Lasswell 1959, It. trans. 1972, p. 252). Hence, the logical conclusion that "the process in question includes, as the reader will have noticed, both communication and collaboration" (ibid., p. 253).

Communication and collaboration: two social dynamics that, from those years onward, became the dominant (if not, sometimes, oppressive) perspective of every investigation into human action and production, even the most intimate and personal.

In this new type of approach, the conditions for the existence of a creative phenomenon depend on the context not only as far as its start-up phase is concerned: they are also decisive in its final phase, in the phase of its evaluation. The social context intervenes in this final phase as it sets the measurement parameters and thus establishes what is to be considered already in the public domain and what, on the other hand, not being so, can be considered creative: therefore "it could be defined as the validating context of the creative process" (Neresini 1994, p. 199). For this reason, therefore, individual judgments cannot be considered valid or sufficient: creativity also forms intersubjectively, "as a result of the interaction between the experiences of individual social actors" (Pedroni 2005, p. 459). We are moving toward a vision of the process that shifts toward "reception" as the central phase of creative production, a shift for which the recognition of originality is primarily based on the judgment of the end user: "An artifact's originality and the artificer's creativity are thus matters of public judgment" (Dasgupta 2019, p. 32).

This state of affairs consequently is also inevitably accompanied by unpleasant consequences, often evoked with tones tinged with scandal and dejection in equal measure: even the recognition of creativity, to varying degrees, whether we accept it or not, "depends on the outcome of the struggles within the field's network of power relations" (Nakamura and Csikszentmihalyi 2003, p. 189).

Yet, there is a very immediate aspect that makes the reasonableness of a collective evaluation of the value of a creative gesture understandable: without shared indications at the interpersonal level, individuals will find themselves in the condition of being able to compare their ideas "to a yardstick that they generate based on their own past experiences" (Reiter-Palmon and Illies 2004, p. 69). If we stop at the subjective perception of the creative experience, the creator can be (legitimately) considered the "appropriate" judge: "After all, who knows the artificer's personal history better than herself?" (Dasgupta 2019, p. 35). Clearly there is nothing worrying about this situation, on the contrary: for the newborn every gesture is innovative, precisely because of the lack of previous personal experiences and, as we will see, we should do everything to preserve this innate, naive ability. But how is it possible when previous experiences increase?

I would like to take this opportunity, at this point, to share an episode from my childhood (I was about 5 or 6 years old), which remained for half a century in a corner of my memory. I remember that one day I built a strange machine with Lego constructions, it had wheels, but it was not attributable to any existing vehicle. Excited about the result, I decided that I should give it a worthy name: I called it Pic Nic. For several days I was proud of both the new creation and the name specially invented for it, so much so that I often repeated it in my head: it was a hypnotic and mysterious sound. Until one evening, on television, I heard a character pronounce exactly the fateful sounds: "Would you like to have a picnic with me?" At first, I wondered who in my house could have "spilled the beans" and, second, what sense could it make for two adults to try to emulate (together) my wheel machine. It was mom who explained the mystery to me, but for a while I did not accept that narrative, continuing to believe that it was a blatant case of plagiarism of intellectual work.

I have brought up this personal memory for two reasons: our creativity uses everything that is given to us (tradition) even unconsciously (who knows where I had heard that sound, which then became "my creature"). The second aspect to remember is that, in the absence of a rich social life, in a narrow circle, there is a risk of considering new what others have already long thought and experienced. A second quality that we have established, in fact, is the "usefulness" of the creative gesture, which "must have some value for a group or a culture" (Hernández-Torrano and Ibrayeva 2020, p. 2). Being creative "always means being creative for someone (person, group, society) at a particular time and place" (Glăveanu 2010, p. 90).

This aspect, however, needs to be clarified, precisely in order not to impair or stifle the innate creative drive that is perhaps the most precious energy of our natural equipment.

2.1.4   The "Unresolved" Gesture

At this point, it is necessary to delve into a delicate theme rarely addressed in the literature I have consulted. Is the dynamics of (social) recognition necessary for the definition of processes, relationships, self-assertions? More precisely, is a creative gesture not recognized by anyone other than its creative creator? Schubert's Unfinished Symphony literally remained in the drawer for about 40 years, before being performed publicly for the first time long after the composer's death: the question is, was it a masterpiece even before? Does posthumous creativity become such only when it is recognized? We could broaden the field of examples to other not specifically artistic sectors: is an intuited and unspoken truth not true? Is an affection felt and never expressed, nothing? If a discovery is not shared, does that prevent it from being defined as such? Is an identity "for oneself" not recognized by others illusory?

When answering, it is important to clarify the distinction between the concept of creativity and that of "creative success," which is evidently of a social nature, is assessable intersubjectively and "is best measured by its reception. For Simonton, 'unrecognized genius becomes an oxymoron'" (Fleming et al. 2007, p. 450). But precisely, we are dealing with two different objects.

I do not think I am able to answer the questions posed exhaustively: I can only state that this issue perhaps leads us to consider an even deeper aspect of the structure and human condition, which I believe to be the expectation, the ultimate wait for any conscious or unconscious gesture (which, among other things, rarely achieves the goal). I take a stand: is a solitary gesture creative? Yes. Because, as we will see, it is the gesture of the child, for whom everything is new and also, I would dare to say, valid and appreciable. Therefore, from his point of view (from the perspective of his consciousness) seeing a cow (let's say) and being amazed, the child is creative in trying to connect this new being to what he already knows, regardless of the social repercussions of this personal achievement.

Once again, poetry with its specific heuristic tools can help us understand this anthropologically "natural" state of affairs. The Italian poet Giovanni Pascoli was expert in describing what he called the "poetics of the child": "There is a little boy inside us. … Child, who cannot reason except in your own way, a childish way that is called profound, because all at once, without making us descend one by one the steps of thought, it transports us into the abyss of truth … you are the eternal child, who sees everything with wonder, everything as if for the first time" (G. Pascoli, *The Eternal Child*, 1897). It is also true that in general, people, becoming adults, continue to produce interesting ideas, many of which, however, are already known to other people, even though they are new to the creator. In this case Margaret Boden speaks of people who are ""psychologically" or "personally" creative: P-creative, for short" (Boden 2009, p. 237). The creative attitude (which we will discuss) is therefore not necessarily "social": others may have already created what we have achieved with effort and creativity, "but this does not dilute or diminish her personal cognitive achievement" (Dasgupta 2019, p. 28).

However, I would like to take a further step, which is not limited to the psychological dimension of this "daily" creativity and is instead able to complete the statement I made earlier, more exhaustively and convincingly, by applying a relational perspective: a solitary gesture can be creative, but it is always "unresolved." It is a "creativity in search of an author" (in this I am perhaps approaching psychoanalytic theories of lack), or rather in search of the fertilizing presence of a recipient. Consciously or not, the creative act is an attempt to establish a strong, reassuring, meaningful bond with the concrete and mysterious reality that surrounds us, especially at its most mysterious level, that is, the human being.

I should therefore conclude that recognition is not just the "condition" for the attribution of the status of "creativity": it is, rather and more precisely, the "aspiration" of every creative act, which cannot be reduced to simple "progress" (unless, with this term, we also want to indicate an increase in the "quality" of human relationships). To fully understand the sense and deep aspiration of the creative impulse (an energy usable in the face of any pro-vocation of reality), it is necessary to make the logical leap of not stopping at its (undisputed and necessary) instrumental functions: creativity (generation) is underpinned by an ultimately relational urgency.

In artistic creation this appears more evident (even if one can make art trying to disregard it):

> The work of art recomposes a unanimity that welds together again the fragments of a divided humanity, not in an absurd and vague idea of man, but in a feasible participation and communication, in which our freedom can find its place. And, reciprocally, when he has composed a work, the artist seems to include himself in an invisible community. [...] This fraternity becomes unattainable takes the form of a creative and effective attitude, but as nostalgia for a lost communion, as a forbidden dream, incessantly revived by an irrepressible desire for emotional fusion (Duvignaud 1967, It. trans. 1969, p. 11 and p. 62).

What Duvignaud called "aesthetics of absolute communion," as an attempt to fill a "violent need for unsatisfied participation," is extendable, in my opinion, to every attempt at creative action by humans, well beyond the boundaries of artistic production.

More recently, using very similar metaphors, it has been stated that the great enterprise of the artist is to transform others and themselves into a new form, gathering everyone in a new shared reality: therefore, as the bridge unites the opposite banks of the river, joining lives in continuous movement, "so the creative person throws a bridge over otherness to gather what is foreign into a new belonging" (Hofstadter 2009, p. 211).

At this point, having tentatively clarified an "inclusive" proposal of the origins and purposes of the creative drive, like Lasswell we can ask ourselves: "What are the elements that facilitate certain innovations? And what elements hinder others?" (Lasswell 1959, It. trans. 1972, p. 255).

One last warning before proceeding to examine the factors favoring or, on the contrary, hindering the development of creativity: sociology has often been entangled in the false problem of the "dimensions" of the phenomena it studies, often considering exclusively events that have numerically significant social repercussions, of mass. It is an understandable error because normally sociologists are asked to provide information and indications on phenomena that involve the highest possible number of cases. The risk, however, is that of neglecting events that happen on a small scale and considering them significant only when they eventually explode (think of the sociological importance of Jeff Bezos' and Steve Jobs' garages or Mark Zuckerberg's Harvard dorm room): a creative gesture (following our previous statement) is "complete" when even a single recipient recognizes it as such. The evaluation of at least one other subject (similar and different) allows the creative gesture to fulfill its *mission*, to avoid the condemnation of being "unresolved."

2.2   Primary Socialization

I will now identify the social components of creativity, that is, the set of environmental conditions capable of promoting (or not) a creative approach to the problems of existence. If we use a chronological criterion, we must acknowledge that most scholars indicate our entry into the world (birth and childhood) as the moment when our propensity for creativity (as happens for all other propensities) receives a sort of ancestral mark that tends to remain stable for the rest of our life: from birth, "the physical and social context participates in the cognitive, social and emotional development of the child: interactions with the social context can socially promote or hinder the creative development" (Mouchiroud and Bernoussi 2008, p. 375).

For this reason, the contexts in which children operate, play, and live can encourage or discourage their full expression of creativity. The family plays a central role in making "normal," and therefore stable, a general basic attitude toward the relationship with things and problems: it "is a critically important influence on and quite possibly the major force behind the etiology of creative behavior" (Kemple and Nissenberg 2000, p. 67). Creativity therefore emerges first and foremost in a relationship "between mother and child" (Glăveanu 2010, p. 85).

For this reason, many studies have been dedicated to profiling the relational and educational "styles" that characterize different contexts of socialization in which the young begin to become aware of things and of themselves.

It has thus been observed, for example, that the family context can stimulate or hinder their children's progressive independence, providing or not the freedom and psychological support necessary to explore, experiment and make decisions, take risks, express their own ideas and feelings without censorship: the choices of parents, their way of approaching reality and the demands or orders established toward their children have a great influence on the future attitude of young people especially toward what is defined as "risk-taking." This attitude is a starting condition for any creative move, since if something new needs to be discovered (aiming at the future), the category of "guarantee" can only rely on what is previous, old, past.

Among the numerous investigations (also empirical) carried out in recent decades aimed at identifying these family educational variables favoring creativity, some even border on eccentricity (so much has the "creative mania" of the West developed): it has been shown, for example, that younger siblings may be more inclined to more creative forms of expression. Unlike firstborns, subsequent children have more opportunities to experiment with interactions with their siblings during their years of development; this difference "can provide them with greater opportunities to negotiate and behave creatively" (Mouchiroud and Bernoussi

2008, p. 375). Similarly, this line of investigation has led to evaluating the influence of the imbalance in the "physical" relationship between siblings, concluding that the younger children tend to turn earlier toward verbal (more creative?) rather than physical topics in conflict resolution.

Research focused on the family context and cognitive development has then highlighted the importance of adequately considering the relationship between educational/training styles and the socio-economic status of the family, leading to a well-developed line of study in the sociology of education: in this case, however, if it is true that the children of wealthy families enjoy more "opportunities" for creative approaches (the Theory of cultural deprivation) being able to draw on diversified and highly qualified sources, it is also true that less affluent family contexts generate situations that produce the necessity of finding solutions, thus affecting (mostly unintentionally) a fundamental factor for the drive to creativity, "motivation." The concept of the *self-made man* envisages a "disadvantaged" start, overcome precisely thanks to the strength of mind that finds ways out, searches for solutions that would not be sought were there no difficulties to be overcome.

Following the lines of this last consideration, scholars have drawn up a list of creative-genetic family conditions. They have found that creative individuals are not usually firstborns, are intellectually precocious, suffer from childhood traumas, their families tend to be economically and socially marginal or both, receive special training early in life and benefit from role models and tutors. There are reservations about the solidity of these results.

The now classic reflection on the social starting conditions of future creatives was accompanied in the 1960s by the classic tripartite recapitulation of educational styles, published by Kurt Lewin, Ron Lippit, and Robert White, of the *Jowa University*, in their famous *Study of Leadership Styles* (1939). The three styles (originally conceived to describe the attitudes of teachers) were applied to parents to evaluate the different creative outcomes in their children: the "Authoritarian" parents, therefore, are those who rely on coercive techniques to discipline the child and show a low level of care for their young. "Permissive" parents set fewer limits on their child's behavior. "Democratic" parents clearly communicate expectations and the reasons for rules, set precise but reasonable limits on their child's behavior, and show a high degree of care. The child who grows up in an authoritarian context, according to these studies, lacks originality and creativity: on the contrary, the parents of creative children are interested in their children's behavior, but do not rely on rigid and immutable rules to control it. Instead, they guarantee their children wide margins of freedom, allowing them to make mistakes, in order to learn from them and overcome them. Adults, in summary, "promote the children's creative development when they allow children to be independent and to take the risks with new and unfamiliar ideas" (Kemple and Nissenberg 2000, p. 68).

In the transition to secondary socialization, more or less the same dynamic is repeated; the teacher (and in later years the professor) becomes the formative subject: schools can provide children with "contexts that allow democratic decisions, like those proposed in alternative educational programs" (Mouchiroud and Bernoussi 2008, p. 375) or deprive them of such a context.

The social status of the family can also have significant repercussions on the development of creativity from childhood onward, both inside and, especially, outside the classroom: "Children from high-status families are more facilitated to participate in extra-curricular activities, which, it is thought, in turn have an impact on the development of creativity" (ibid.).

2.3   Motivation

Why dedicate a space to the theme of motivation in a study on creativity? And above all, why put this analysis in a chapter that concerns the social components of the creative attitude?

To answer the first question, take a look at the existing interdisciplinary scientific literature: many scholars argue that a high "intrinsic" motivation, that which an individual commits "for the love of the activity itself" (Baer et al. 2003, p. 569), is a necessary ingredient to promote creativity.

While the definition is rich and fascinating, and at the same time enigmatic (what does "love for the activity itself" mean?), the critical point is the "management" of the magical ingredient: in fact, so fundamental is the presence of this energy that a new professional figure (as well-paid as the required skills are nebulous)[2], the "motivator," has emerged, (!). It is therefore a push toward creativity that can only be personal, but that is affected by the stimuli of the environment. It follows that the answer to the second question is that motivation is partly the result of an initiative of the subject and partly the consequence of a particular "cultural" influence of the social context in which one operates.

The next question has to be: what culture is being developed today to achieve the development and continuity of this fundamental energy for the increase of every human activity? We could introduce the response to this with a general statement: the invitation to be creative today is based on reasons that can be generically defined as "instrumental" (*primarily* for economic purposes) and this, in the long run, inevitably ends up wearing out and drying up the most intimate sources of the creative drive. In practice, within organizations, motivation simply comes to occupy "the hegemonic role that was first of control" (De Masi 2003, p. 668).

Essentially, it was psychology that highlighted some relational and contextual characteristics that favor a creative approach, especially, if not exclusively (a limit of many investigations), in the workplace: the reasons for this choice can be understood, but this situation already suggests that these will be "sectoral" motivations, which pragmatically stimulate creativity in specific situations, without worrying about intersecting the underlying, original motivation of the operator.

To therefore promote the development of these "feelings," scholars of organizational processes have insisted greatly on the "type" of activity in which the individual engages, implicitly stating that the creative attitude depends on the characteristics of "what you do." It thus becomes reasonable to expect that complex jobs (i.e., those characterized by high levels of autonomy, variety of skills, identity, importance, and feedback) encourage higher levels of intrinsic motivation and creativity compared to jobs

---

[2] "These 'creativity trainers' are missionaries of the 'American model.' Often lacking solid scientific foundations, they subject well-paying students to whimsical psychophysical exercises, deluding them that an undiscovered genius lurks in their brain; they transform creativity, that most mysterious and precious expression of the human species, into a sideshow phenomenon" (De Masi 2003, p. 672).

of a relatively simple and routine nature. When jobs are complex, individuals are more easily motivated and "interested in performing them for the love of the activity itself—conditions that lead to creativity at work" (Baer et al. 2003, p. 572).

For the same reason, jobs that are simpler and routinized may not motivate employees or allow them the flexibility to try new paths, take risks, and operate creatively. It is necessary to ask, then, whether the job is "designed to be sufficiently challenging to motivate individuals to be creative" (Shalley and Gilson 2004, p. 37). From here, logically, a race to make work activity as non-routine as possible, to provide variety in tasks, etc. There are several long-established methods for "shuffling the deck" in an anti-routine function: one of these is job rotation. In some Japanese companies (see Seiko), for example, a prerequisite for career advancement is having done many job rotations, another strategy is voluntary temporary assignment to different departments with incentives such as bonuses, or finally the creation of "'mixer' opportunities" (Maruyama 2003, p. 609).

Another element carefully observed is that of the "objectives" of individual operations: they are the ones that increase attention and effort when the goals toward which individuals can direct their energies are clear. It is the sharing of objectives that stimulates attention in the workplace, determines the tenacity and duration of effort, and stimulates efforts toward the discovery of more effective strategies in order to achieve the goals. Goals are more easily achieved when they coincide with the personal ambitions of the worker, when positive feedback rewards proactive attitudes. When employees do not know what the organization wants, because clear objectives are not given, "they felt lower levels of creativity resulted" (Shalley and Gilson 2004, p. 38).

These are evidently facilitating strategies, which, however, as we have mentioned, risk settling at a middle level, not going to the roots: this explains, for example, the fact that, in different cultural contexts, one can even hypothesize the opposite, as Émile Durkheim argued more than a century ago. The French sociologist was very critical of the belief of many entrepreneurs or institutional leaders in the need for what he called "vast horizons," "overall visions," "beautiful generalities": if the worker gets used to this vastness of consciousness, he no longer lets himself to be confined "without impatience" within the narrow limits of a specific task. The division of social labor certainly assumes that the worker does not limit himself to his small, solitary task, that he does not lose sight of his collaborators and that he interacts with them. Certainly, the worker is not and should not become a machine that repeats movements whose objectives he does not understand: he must know that they serve to achieve a goal of some kind. He must be aware, in summary, "of serving a purpose." But no more than that. It is not necessary for him to be aware of the entirety of the social horizon in which he operates: it is sufficient that he discerns enough to understand that his actions "have a purpose that goes beyond them. From then on, his activity, however specific and uniform, is the activity of an intelligent being, because it has a meaning and he knows it" (Durkheim 1893, It. trans. 1962, pp. 363–364).

Knowing that one's actions "have a purpose that goes beyond them": this would be the key to a proactive and creative attitude. However, if we want to share this definition, we are also forced to ask ourselves: toward or until where? For Durkheim this transcendence (from the most daily to the transcendental, i.e., religious) is a product of society: therefore, in the end, everything falls back into the circle of socio-cultural conventions in which one operates. Thus, we have not managed to dissect the concept of "love for the activity itself" from which we started.

Paradoxically, as current psychology teaches us, motivations of this kind may sooner or later come up against the dead end of the so-called *over-justification effect*, an effect of overmotivation, for which, in the case of a rewarding activity, any external rewards paradoxically end up weakening the intrinsic motivation, "externalizing" it in the reward. Concrete gratifications, therefore, "not only do not encourage, but risk achieving the opposite effect" (Tomasello 2009, It. trans. 2010, p. 26).

Biological sciences can offer an interesting starting point for strategies capable of opposing these regressive effects: bringing up the unconscious (a novelty, for the years in which the concepts that follow were expressed), it began to be thought that incentives are needed to build something new, i.e., a purpose is needed to achieve (and, so far, this is nothing new). The promising aspect of this approach is linked to the declension of this original and universal dynamic in function of a kind of goal that is much less concrete than, for example, the search for food, a mate, promotion, enjoyment, pleasure: some scholars have begun to explore the necessity and irreplaceability of creative energy especially in the presence of something that is still "rudimentary," "formless," something that tries to express itself. The urgency and the drive to artistic expressiveness, for example, would be born exactly at this level that in which there are only vague hints or nebulous sketches in the mind. Often this anxious search is accompanied by inner struggles that leave the would-be creator exhausted and undone; "But when he abandons it, the lower levels of his spirit, the unconscious ones, continue it and in many cases with good success" (Sinnott 1959, It. trans. 1972, p. 47).

A different perspective is emerging from this description; a perspective that is not instrumental that ignores declared or conscious objectives. It has its origins in something "formless" that seeks for expression and that does not care, ultimately, about the effects of its own commitment.

A few years ago Richard Sennet devoted much attention to this *modus operandi* typical of the *craftsman*, the artisan, a wealth of tradition that risks being lost: for the American sociologist the carpenter, the laboratory technician, and the orchestra conductor are all craftsmen, because for them a piece of work being well-done is important for its own sake. They perform a practical activity, but their work is not simply a means to achieve an end of another order. The "ethics of well-done work," for the simple pleasure of doing it well, typical of the craftsman, today "is not rewarded or even noticed" (Sennett 2008, It. trans. 2009, pp. 27 and 43).

In this regard, the profound insights of the French poet Charles Peguy come to mind:

> Once upon a time, workers were not slaves. They worked. They cultivated an absolute honor, as befits an honor. The leg of a chair had to be well made. It was natural, it was understood. It was a priority. It didn't need to be well made for the wage, or in proportion to the wage. It didn't have to be well made for the master, nor for the connoisseurs, nor for the master's customers. It had to be well made for itself, in itself, in its very nature. A tradition that came, risen from the depths of the race, a history, an absolute, an honor demanded that chair leg be well made. And every part of the chair was well made. And every part of the chair that was not seen was worked with the same perfection as the parts that were seen. According to

the same principle of the cathedrals. And it's only me—I now so bastard-ized—to make it so long now. For them, in them there was not even the shadow of a reflection. The work was there. They worked well. It was not about being seen or not being seen. It was the work itself that had to be well done (Peguy 1913, It. trans. 1991).

"According to the same principle of the cathedrals": a few years ago, I happened to visit the cathedral of Chartres (much beloved by the French poet). The guide informed us of the significance of the experience of climbing the bell tower: it was, in fact, a privilege reserved for a lucky few, since for many centuries access to the towers had been forbidden. Climbing the steps, I thought to myself: "The decorations that were placed here would not have been seen by anyone and whoever made them knew it." Therefore, following my exquisitely economic mentality I thought I would find in the back of the tower (the part not visible from below, above the roof of the cathedral at a height of over 100 m) the less pleasing *gargoyles*, the ones with defects. It was a great embarrassment, turning the corner, to find myself face to face with a monkey carved in stone with a wealth of details, who was watching me as if making fun of me, perfect, without defects.

What I am delving into here opens a further perspective of investigation, focusing on the delicate relationship existing between intrinsic motivation and identity construction: Morris Eagle speaks in this case of "genuine interests" which, exactly like creative activities, require to be pursued autonomously, for themselves rather than for external purposes, among which the American psychologist unexpectedly also considers those aimed at supporting and maintaining the functioning of the *ego*. The somewhat paradoxical fact is then clarified by stating that if one pursued interests in order to seek support for the ego, they would no longer be authentic interests: only if one pursues interests in themselves, for love, "they can be considered genuine interests and are able to constitute supports for the ego" (Eagle 2013, p. 23).

Culture has a great influence in promoting work well done and its motivations or, conversely, its unstable imitation: today it seems that an investment in the second strategy is more widespread, because it is more rewarding than the first. Therefore, no room should be left for possible individualistic interpretations of intrinsic motivation, interpretations that, under false pretenses, would paradoxically lead to the affirmation of new forms of pure and radical instrumentality or of narcissism under false pretenses.

Creative action, in fact, "challenges the separation between the self and the other" (Glăveanu 2018, p. 29). If intrinsic motivation has been recognized by many as a precious source of creative energies, research so far has produced ambivalent results: for this reason, some scholars argue that the relationship between intrinsic motivation and creativity is enhanced by "psychological processes focused on the other. A perspective-taking generated by prosocial motivation encourages the development of ideas that are useful as well as new" (Grant and Berry 2011, p. 73). The "prosocial" motivation (the desire to benefit others) is therefore considered complementary to the intrinsic one, correcting its possible distortions: it has been observed, in fact, that in some cases, rather than provoking creativity, the productions of intrinsic motivation "could derive from greater enjoyment and satisfaction experienced in expressing creativity" (Amabile et al. 1986, p. 21).

It is important to note that, starting from the 1990s, research (especially American) has increasingly focused on the growing phenomenon of the "third sector," highlighting aspects which non-profit companies can teach to those which operate for profit. Observing the activities that were carried out in those years in environments supported by volunteers (churches, hospitals, orchestras, museums, universities, Red Cross, Salvation Army, Boy-scouts, etc.), a vertiginous increase in efficiency was recorded just when the performance of human resources was decreasing in large companies. In creative groups, as in "third sector" organizations, there is a strong tension toward the mission which is given "priority over everything else." The mission is taken as an operational reference point, as a guide to action and as a parameter of evaluation: "Volunteering and disinterest constitute the main spring of belonging" (De Masi 2003, p. 661).

It has therefore been concluded that intrinsic motivation, while it is fundamental in the field of artistic creativity, writing, and solving business problems, in other applications it guides the production of ideas that are certainly new, but not necessarily useful: it has been noted, for example, that "many intrinsically motivated architects had difficulty producing creative ideas because they were focused on the novelty of their projects" (Grant and Berry 2011, p. 75). Prosocial motivation (this term could be translated as "relational") would therefore be able to improve the impact of intrinsic motivation on creativity by providing the stimulus to "engage based on the concern to help or support other people. [...] In this way, our research presents a new relational view of creativity" (ibid., pp. 77 and 91).

2.4 Leadership and Creativity

"In order for creativity to occur, leadership needs to play an active role" (Shalley and Gilson 2004, p. 35). Among the social components of creativity, we must therefore consider the quality of the asymmetric relationship existing between leaders and followers. Also in this case, we must register a potential and practiced reductionist temptation of what we tend to call "authoritative relationship": the linguistic strategy of using the term "leadership" instead of "authority" signals, on the one hand, the prevalence of professional and work approaches to creativity studies, and, on the other, the strong pragmatic imprint of the English term, which relieves the relationship in question from uncomfortable moral obligations to settle on the less problematic ground of effectiveness, but with the risk of losing interesting opportunities along the way.

The investigations born within work contexts and aimed at improving their productivity and competitiveness focus on various aspects related to the management of authority in promoting or, on the contrary, hindering the creativity of employees: hence, among the main positive functions of the role that leaders play in facilitating the creative production of their subordinates is their responsibility to promote, within the work context, a culture attentive to "the climate of the organization and to the "perception of support for innovation" (Reiter-Palmon and Illies 2004, p. 56), that is, making the climate, environment, and practices (i.e., rewards, incentives, objectives, and expected evaluations) "such that creative outcomes can and do occur" (Shalley and Gilson 2004, p. 35).

Another topic explored by numerous empirical research studies is the relationship between leader behavior and employee creativity: these have been established that creativity is higher when managers listen to their employees' ideas and ask for their advice in decisions that concern them; that negative feedback from leaders inhibits scientific creativity; that sharing in the problem-building phases and feelings of self-efficacy lead to greater employee creativity; that open interactions with supervisors and receiving encouragement and support lead to increasing employee creativity.

There are also more specific studies on the fact that the different "brokerage" arrangements that can be created may affect greater collaborative creativity: when subject A has ties with subjects B and C, if there is no link between B and C, an "open network" is formed; a link between B and C, on the other hand, would make it a "closed network." Closed networks, according to some scholars, promote mutual trust based on direct knowledge and this should result in a better flow of information compared to open networks. Since creative efforts generally benefit from new information, a better flow of information should improve creativity. However, in open networks, ties tend to be weaker and more likely to connect people with different interests and perspectives. The so-called *brokers* (intermediaries) occupy the most advantageous position being at the intersection of different information sources: thanks to this position, therefore, they are the ones who have "the best opportunity to generate new combinations" (Fleming et al. 2007, p. 445).

All of this, confirmed by empirical data, remains a source of practical indications of great value: its very merit, however, its performativity, can be read as a limit, failing to transcend the entirely legitimate constraint of instrumentality. Creativity obtained in this way turns out to be something that can gladly be gotten rid of as soon as the context that strategically values and rewards it is left behind. I think (due to in-depth studies on the authoritative relationship) that something more can be expected (also from the point of view of operational returns) from this structurally asymmetric interaction between who leads and who follows in terms of support for the creative attitude.

In the mid-1970s, an article was published by three American psychologists (Jerome Bruner, David Wood, and Gail Ross) who highlighted (with empirical results) that the most effective way to teach a child to solve problems—in their case "creatively" building a pyramid using small wooden blocks—is to "scaffold" his activity, until such operation proves unnecessary: *to scaffold* indeed means to support an operational situation (e.g., in construction) through supports, which, once the task is completed, must be dismantled. In the educational field, the English term has been understood as "a form of 'vicarious consciousness' provided by an adult for the benefit of a younger student" (Littleton 2013, p. 52).

The three psychologists, retracing the path previously traced by the Russian psychologist and pedagogue Lev Vygotsky, used the metaphor of *scaffolding* precisely to describe how educators can provide more assistance to students "within the Zone of Proximal Development to help them move towards independence" (Smit et al. 2012, p. 820). Radically revisiting the methods of transmitting elementary principles of *problem solving* and acquiring skills to children, the three authors critically judged the usual premise that envisages the young student isolated and without assistance: "fending for oneself" is not always the best method to really get by. The intervention of a tutor must involve something more: the process of "scaffolding" must allow the young person the possibility of solving a problem, carrying out a task or achieving a goal that would be beyond his capabilities, if not assisted. This scaffolding must be provided by an adult who performs the function of "control" from above, through the management of those elements of the task that are initially beyond the student's capacity, "thus allowing him to focus on the elements and complete only those that are within his *range* of competences" (Wood et al. 1976, p. 90).

As can be inferred, the success of this procedure has two preliminary conditions: the first consists in giving priority to the learning process according to the potential abilities present in the young person compared to the ability to apply theories and strategies present in the teacher; the second condition is that the tutor demonstrates a marked sensitivity in understanding "which" skills the child already possesses and, based on these, which he could acquire in a certain educational path. In summary, well-executed scaffolding begins with attracting the child to actions that produce "recognizable-for-him" solutions. Then the tutor can show the discrepancies of the path taken and finally assume "a role of confirmation until the assisted person is enabled to fly alone" (ibid. p. 96).

Ultimately, it is an effective methodology thanks to its synergy with the most elementary dynamics of learning: social psychology teaches that people's experience settles into routine practices, orders, and regulations that constitute a scaffolding of stability, becoming a sort of "hard core" of what will then be experienced as non-problematic, as taken for granted. Routines (which we can consider the basic ground on which to then begin the real adventure of social creativity) necessarily imply a partly creative and partly instrumental communication and require "a recurring but transitory time commitment, and once the action is completed it does not involve further reflections" (Emiliani 2008, pp. 187 and 199).

When you manage to create an educational context with these characteristics, the adult-child interaction is subject to a constant re-definition of the situation by the two participating subjects within an ever-increasing "intersubjectivity": as the child masters the task, the adult decreases the extent of his assistance while remaining on the border of a continuous expansion of the child's competence. In this way, the progressive transition from the interpsychological to the intrapsychological level takes place, which involves a progressive and constant decrease in the adult's interventions: basically, the adult must transit from doing the action for the child to providing directions on how to do the action to mere supervision, "as children grasp the functional meaning of the actions performed" (Pontecorvo 1999, pp. 56–58).

In summary, the educator indicates the path, then lets the student proceed ahead of him for new explorations; he provides suggestions to avoid missteps or mishaps; knowing the end of the journey, he guides the student, always leaving open the choice of the itinerary. The educator must assume the responsibility of his function, without distorting it with excesses of authority, without continuing it when it is no longer useful. His action must be "temporary": he is in that position to overcome a stage. Then he must disappear. The child, the teenager, "will continue his journey, either with another guide, or autonomously" (Postic 1979, It. trans. 1994, p. 120). Therefore, while the leader or teacher must know how to attract and involve, even more important is knowing when to withdraw, "to disappear without the group crumbling under the weight of mourning or the feeling of impotence" (De Masi 2003, p. 670).

The phase of "disappearance" is the fundamental element and the final stage of the scaffolding process as it highlights a very particular way of using power and educational authority: the progressive decrease of teacher control, as soon as the students demonstrate understanding and mastery of practices, is made possible through "fading" and the "transfer of responsibility." The phase of "handing over" for independence, the ultimate goal of the scaffolding process, clearly documents the temporary nature of the scaffolding: the temporary nature of the educational relationship is respected when it comes to recognizing operationally that "the handover (effective) is a process that includes fading of teacher support" (Smit et al. 2012, p. 821).

This temporariness of the guiding function and the discovery made goes well beyond the learning processes typical of the early stages of life: science too must move respecting these coordinates having as a guideline the existence of a "given" reality, intersubjectively recordable, eternally inexhaustible and exceeding every stage of new knowledge: the scientist's research presupposes the existence of an external reality, according to Michael Polanyi. It starts from this "given," the search for a hidden truth toward which the clues point; and when the discovery finally ends the research, "its validity is sustained by a vision of reality pointing further beyond it" (Polanyi 2009, p. 162).

A research relationship (elementary, practical, or scientific) based on these pedagogical cornerstones is perhaps the most precious source of education for creativity, as an attitude toward reality and not just as a tool for professional and social climbing however this is an infrequent dynamic, not at all taken for granted, which needs to be bolstered by an ideal, almost revolutionary, force capable of opposing the powerful *mainstream* of the instrumental approach.

It means, in other words, strongly supporting the primacy of the person over his products: promoting creativity, in this sense, means accepting the individual as an "unconditional value." The leader promotes creativity when he recognizes that the individual entrusted to him for whatever reason or situation represents "a value in itself." This also happens when the teacher, the parent, or whosoever for them perceives the potential of the child and, consequently, "is able to have in him an unconditional trust, whatever the conditions of the moment" (May 1959, It. trans. 1972, p. 106).

During the recent *International Conference on Trust* at the *Institute of Social Sciences* in Tokyo in which I had the pleasure of participating, Prof. Bart Nooteboom (*Faculty of Economics and Business Administration*, Tilburg University, The Netherlands) made a very interesting reference to a new model of worker emerging forcefully in our production systems using the expression, "*Isolated and fully monitored professionals.*" He asked at this point: "*Is there any need for trust left?*" The answer, which is relevant to this investigation, is precisely related to the risks for creativity when trust is lacking: *No creativity without trust.*

This "unconditional trust" is perhaps the most essential relational condition to support the weight of the dark side of every creative endeavor: the risk. Creativity implicitly involves "risks": to develop new and useful products or processes, "individuals have to be willing to try and to possibly fail" (Shalley and Gilson 2004, p. 36). The famous American basketball player, Michael Jordan, expressed this unwelcome but essential ingredient of "failure" with a pithy phrase that is widely circulated on the internet: "I've missed more than 9,000 shots in my career. I've lost more than 300 games. Twenty-six times I've been trusted to take the game-winning shot and missed. I've failed over and over again in my life. And that's why I've succeeded." No one can relieve a person from the straits of risk and possible failure, because in that case, they would no longer be creative. An authoritative or simply personal relationship, however, can guarantee human and also psychological support to resist the temptation to withdraw from the venture before "having tried."

I shall conclude this section observing that the support dynamic we investigated as the most suitable methodology to develop children's creativity retains its validity (with appropriate expressiveness and modalities) even when the child becomes an adult; there is a social development that can be derived from this observation, i.e., that adult creativity, not just individual but collective, can in turn be supported through a "subsidiary" policy, i.e., capable of scaffolding the bottom-up attempt to respond creatively to the needs that a group of people find themselves sharing. The theme of "civil creativity" should perhaps be resumed with courageous policies of civil, social, administrative, and political *scaffolding*, in which public institutions should attempt, at a certain point, to apply the hoped-for *fading*.

References

Amabile T.M., Hennessey B.A., Grossman B.S. (1986), *Social influences on creativity: The effects of contracted-for reward*, in "Journal of Personality and Social Psychology", 50: 14-23.

Appadurai A. (2004), *The Capacity to Aspire: Culture and the Terms of Recognition*, Stanford, Calif.: Stanford University Press: Stanford Social Sciences, It. trans. *Le aspirazioni nutrono la democrazia*, et al./edizioni, Milano, 2011.

Arbiser S. (2004), *Il gruppo interno come modello della mente*, in "Funzionegamma", ottobre, 1 – 26.

Baer M., Oldham G.R., Cummings A. (2003), *Rewarding creativity: when does it really matter?*, in "The Leadership Quarterly" 14: 569 – 586.

Bauman Z. (2012), *Conversazioni sull'educazione*, Erickson, Trento.

Boden M.A. (2009), *Creativity: how does it Work?*, in Krausz M., Dutton D., Bardsley K. (ed.), *The Idea of Creativity*, Brill, Leiden-Boston.

Briskman L. (2009), *Creative Product and Creative Process in Science and Art*, in Krausz M., Dutton D., Bardsley K. (ed.), *The Idea of Creativity*, Brill, Leiden-Boston.

Dasgupta S. (2019), *A Cognitive Historical Approach to Creativity*, Routledge, London – New York.

De Masi D. (2003), *La fantasia e la concretezza*, Milano, Rizzoli.

Durkheim É. (1893), *De la division du travail social*, Alcan, Paris, It. trans. *La divisione del lavoro sociale*, Edizioni di comunità, Milano 1962.

Duvignaud J. (1967), *Sociologie de l'art*, Presses Universitaires de France, Paris; It. trans. *Sociologia dell'arte*, Il Mulino, Bologna 1969.

Eagle M.N. (2013), *Autonomy & Relatedness: Self-Realization Versus Self-Absorption*, in "Clin. Soc. Work J.", 41: 20-25.

Emiliani F. (2008), *La realtà delle piccole cose*, il Mulino, Bologna.

Federici R. (2006), *Elementi sociologici della creatività. La centralità creativa degli autori del pensiero classico*, FrancoAngeli, Milano.

Fleming L., Mingo S., & Chen D. (2007), *Collaborative Brokerage, Generative Creativity, and Creative Success*, in "Administrative Science Quarterly", 52: 443-475.

Glăveanu V.P. (2010), *Paradigms in the study of creativity: Introducing the perspective of cultural psychology*, in "New Ideas in Psychology", 28: 79-93.

Glăveanu V.P. (2018), *Educating which creativity?*, in "Thinking Skills and Creativity", 27: 25-32.

Glăveanu V.P., et al. (2019), *Advancing Creativity Theory and Research: A Sociocultural Manifesto*, in "The Journal of Creative Behavior", 54(3): 741-745.

Grant A.M., Berry J.W. (2011), *The necessity of others is the mother of invention: Intrinsic and prosocial motivations, perspective taking, and creativity*, in "The Academy of Management Journal", 54(1): 73-96.

Hernández-Torrano D., Ibrayeva L. (2020), *Creativity and education: A bibliometric mapping of the research literature (1975–2019)*, in "Thinking Skills and Creativity" 35, 100625.

Hofstadter A. (2009), *On the Dialectical Phenomenology of Creativity*, in Krausz M., Dutton D., Bardsley K. (ed.), *The Idea of Creativity*, Brill, Leiden-Boston.

Katz E., Lazarsfeld P.F. (1955), *Personal influence: The part played by people in the flow of mass communications*, The Free Press, New York.

Kemple K.M., Nissenberg S.A. (2000), *Nurturing Creativity in Early Childhood Education: Families Are Part of It*, in "Early Childhood Education Journal", 28(1).

Lasswell H.D. (1959), *The social development of creativity*, in Anderson H.H. (ed.), *Creativity and its Cultivation*, Harper & Row, New York, It. trans. *La creatività e le sue prospettive*, La scuola, Brescia 1972.

Littleton K. (2013), *Adaptation and authority in scaffolding and teacher–student relationships Commentary on the Special Issue 'Conceptualising and grounding scaffolding in complex educational contexts' Learning*, in "Culture and Social Interaction", 2: 52-55.

Maddalena G. (2021), *Filosofia del gesto*, Carocci, Roma.

Maruyama M. (2003), *Causal Loops, Interaction, and Creativity*, in "International Review of Sociology—Revue Internationale de Sociologie", 13(3).

May R. (1959), *The nature of creativity*, in Anderson H.H. (ed.), *Creativity and its Cultivation*, Harper & Row, New York, It. trans. *La creatività e le sue prospettive*, La scuola, Brescia 1972.

McWilliam E., Dawson S. (2008), *Teaching for creativity: towards sustainable and replicable pedagogical practice*, in "High Education" 56: 633-643.

Mead M. (1959), *La Creativity seen from an intercultural perspective*, in Anderson H.H. (ed.), Creativity and its Cultivation, Harper & Row, New York, It. trans. La creatività e le sue prospettive, La scuola, Brescia 1972.

Melucci A. (1994), *Creatività: miti, discorsi, processi,* in Melucci A. (ed.), *Creatività: miti, discorsi, processi,* Feltrinelli, Milano.

Morin E. (1990), *"Exergue"* a Manghi S., *Il gatto con le ali,* Feltrinelli, Milano.

Mouchiroud C., Bernoussi A. (2008), *An empirical study of the construct validity of social creativity,* in "Learning and Individual Differences" 18: 372 -380.

Murray H.A. (1959), *The vicissitudes of creativity,* in Anderson H.H. (ed.), *Creativity and its Cultivation,* Harper & Row, New York, It. trans. *La creatività e le sue prospettive,* La scuola, Brescia 1972.

Nakamura J., Csikszentmihalyi M. (2003), *Creativity in Later Life,* in SAWYER R.K., et al., *Creativity and development,* Oxford University Press, New York, 186-216.

Neresini F. (1994), *Creatività e contesti: relazioni e istituzioni,* in Melucci A. (ed.), *Creatività: miti, discorsi, processi,* Feltrinelli, Milano.

Pedroni M. (2005), *Genio individuale o pratica sociale? Le mille facce della creatività,* in «Studi di sociologia», 4: 439-461.

Peguy C. (1913), *L'argent,* Cahiers de la Quinzaine, Paris, It. trans. *Il denaro,* Lavoro, Roma 1991.

Polanyi M. (2009), *The Creative Imagination,* in Krausz M., Dutton D., Bardsley K. (ed.), *The Idea of Creativity,* Brill, Leiden-Boston.

Pontecorvo, C. (1999), *Interazione e costruzione della conoscenza: paradigmi a confronto e prospettive di ricerca,* in Pontecorvo, C. – Ajello, A.M. – Zucchermaglio, C., *Discutendo si impara. Interazione sociale e conoscenza a scuola,* Carocci, Roma.

Postic, M. (1979), *La relation educative,* Presses Universitaires de France, Paris, It. trans. *La relazione educativa. Oltre il rapporto maestro-scolaro,* Armando Editore, Roma 1994.

Reiter-Palmon R., Illies J.J. (2004), *Leadership and creativity: Understanding leadership from a creative problem-solving perspective,* in "The Leadership Quarterly", 15: 5- 77.

Reuter M.E. (2015), *Creativity – A Sociological Approach,* Palgrave, London.

Savonardo L. (2010), *Sociologia della musica. La costruzione sociale del suono dalle tribù al digitale,* Utet, Torino.

Sawyer R.K. (2003), *Emergence in Creativity and Development,* in Sawyer R.K., et al., *Creativity and development,* Oxford University Press, New York, pp. 12-60.

Sennett, R. (2008), *The craftsman,* Yale University Press, New Haven, London; It. trans. *L'uomo artigiano,* Feltrinelli, Milano 2009.

Shalley C.E., Gilson L.L. (2004), *What leaders need to know: A review of social and contextual factors that can foster or hinder creativity,* in "The Leadership Quarterly", 15: 33-53.

Sinnott E.W. (1959), *The creativity of life,* in Anderson H.H. (ed.), *Creativity and its Cultivation,* Harper & Row, New York, It. trans. *La creatività e le sue prospettive,* La scuola, Brescia 1972.

Smit J., van Eerde H.A.A., Bakker A. (2012), *A conceptualisation of whole-class scaffolding,* British Educational Research Journal.

Tomasello, M. (2009), *Why we Cooperate,* Massachusetts Institute of Technology, Cambridge, MA; It. trans. *Altruisti nati. Perché cooperiamo fin da piccoli,* Bollati Boringhieri, Torino 2010.

van der Zandena P.J.A.C., Meijera P.C., Beghetto R.A. (2020), *A review study about creativity in adolescence: Where is the social context?,* in "Thinking Skills and Creativity", 38: 100702

Wood D., Bruner J.S. and Ross G. (1976), *The role of tutoring in problem solving,* in "Journal of Child Psychology and Psychiatry", 17: 89-100.

3

The "Creative Processes"

Abstract In Chap. 2 I analyzed the "social" elements of the creative capacity, from the more external to the now "internalized," and now, in this chapter, after having identified the socio-cultural elements that determine (favoring or inhibiting) the development of a creative attitude in the face of reality, I will attempt to identify the fundamental factors of what can be defined as the "creative process": with this expression we mean first of all that creativity is the particular process of moving from state A to state B (process) through unconventional paths.

In this perspective, a number of points must be defined in order to speak of a creative *agency*, i.e., a starting need, a point of arrival that is not always entirely clear, even if always present, and a series of operational steps combined in an original manner, thanks to a particular "attitude" that is defined as "creative," from which we will start to clarify the dynamics of the process. In an ideally consequential pathway, we will reflect on what it means to "creatively place oneself" in front of things; how this placing oneself is necessarily to be understood as a "gesture" (both practical and cognitive); what processes are triggered by this particular type of activity; what challenges today's technology poses to the classical concepts of creative action; and finally the possibility of "educational" strategies linked to the development of creativity.

P. P. Bellini, *The Creative Gesture*, Palgrave Studies in Creativity and Culture,
https://doi.org/10.1007/978-3-031-54219-0_3

71

Keywords Creative attitude • Creative gesture • Divergent thinking •
Construction of the problem • Interdisciplinarity • Randomness •
Synthetic creativity • Training

3.1   The Creative Attitude

To define the creative attitude, I have taken a number of passages of great
descriptive and communicative effectiveness from the intervention of the
well-known psychoanalyst Erich Fromm, a member of the Frankfurt
School, at the American conference of 1959. He proposed a creative
answer to the question: "What are the necessary conditions in the creative attitude?" His reply: "First of all, the ability to be 'perplexed' is
indispensable. Children still retain this ability to feel perplexed. All their
strenuous activity consists in trying to orient themselves in a new world,
to grasp the meaning of the perennially new things they learn through
experience. They are perplexed, surprised, capable of marveling and it is
precisely for this reason that their reaction is creative" (Fromm 1959, It.
trans. p. 72).

This "childlike perplexity" allows children a second great opportunity:
that of being able to live a less "knowledgeable," "cultural," "mediated"
relationship with reality, which is "more" unknown to them than to
adults: they live in the world of nature rather than in that of concepts,
abstractions, beliefs, and stereotypes, a condition that can be effectively
defined as "openness to experience" (May 1959, It. trans. 1972, p. 114).
This openness, which underlies the creative attitude, provides the opportunity, in other words, of somehow resizing, or rather of restoring—without in any way casting a veil of suspicion on its fundamental
importance—the absoluteness of symbolic mediation to its place in
learning processes.

Albeit by different paths, similar conclusions had been reached by the
French philosopher Merleau-Ponty when he stated that man is naturally
inclined to forget "his dimension of being," thus clarifying the critical
point related to the concrete operations that we perform starting from
perception. As acutely observed, we build theories by virtue of experience, but then we "forget" the operations we have performed and confuse

theories with the original reality from which we started to build them. Merleau-Ponty strives to bring the sciences back to the original operations that we tend to forget, highlighting the urgency "to rediscover these operations and to follow their structure to understand their characteristics and internal dynamics" (Paci 2004, p. 11).

This demanding process of "rediscovery," typical of the adult, seems to be the only antidote to the loss of creativity that accompanies the increase in knowledge: the "dimension of being" from which the theories we learned at home or at school desks are born is all in the fact that they were originally practices that were creatively born in the face of concrete problems of existence. Only this backward journey (implicit or explicit) can make theories effective by avoiding their deadly action against our creativity: we tend to lose this ability to be amazed, once we enter the educational process. The idea of having to know everything about a certain field of knowledge leads to considering surprise or perplexity as a sign of ignorance: in this way reality is no longer a world full of wonders and tends to be progressively simply accepted as it is. But in reality "the ability to feel perplexed is the premise of any creation, whether in the artistic or scientific field" (Fromm 1959, It. trans. p. 72).

Freud, on the other hand, thought that the artist was like a child who plays and "creates a world of his own, or rather, rearranges the things of his world in a new way that pleases him" (Freud 1907/1989, p. 437).

Therefore, this "return to childhood" of evangelical memory (already then considered impracticable) turns out to be a complex operation, Yet, although challenging, "adult" creativity can find its reason for being, as another American psychoanalyst illustrated through the case histories of some of his patients: "Almost all children are able to perceive more freely, without a priori expectations of what should be, or what must be, or what has always been. If it is true that children are naive, then I could say that my subjects had arrived at a 'second naivety,' to use Santayana's expression. Their 'innocence' of perception and expressiveness was accompanied by intelligence" (May 1959, It. trans. 1972, p. 114). A "second naivety," adult, capable of being amazed "despite" its knowledge, combining "innocence" with "intelligence."

For artists, this arduous and often painful ascent to the state of initial purity is an onerous task, as Picasso pointed out with some well-known aphorisms: "All children are born artists; the difficult thing is to remain so as adults." "At twelve I painted like Raphael, but it took me a lifetime to learn to paint like a child."

It should be noted that there are critical positions regarding this *naïve* perspective of creativity,[1] especially in relation to the concrete, social context in which creative abilities are used (on this we have already expressed a position using the expression of "unresolved gesture").

To conclude, returning to Fromm, there is a second premise for the creative attitude: it is the ability to "concentrate," now a rare skill in our daily round at least here in the West, where we are constantly busy with no possibility of focusing on something exclusively. While we are doing one thing, we are already thinking about what we will do next and as soon as we can we do several things simultaneously: "We consume breakfast, listen to the radio, read the newspaper and perhaps we also manage to converse with the wife and children. We do five things all at once and we do nothing" (Fromm 1959, It. trans. p. 72). And it must be remembered that Fromm was writing before the development (technological, but consequently anthropological and perceptive) of modern *multitasking* as a daily dynamic of every activity of contemporary man. In this case too, we need to find, urgently, a reconciliation between the technology available and the development and constraints of individual consciousness: today as then, "for those who really concentrate, the thing they are doing at a given moment is the most important in life" (ibid., p. 73).

Finally, also the Swiss psychologist Jean Piaget was interested in the mechanisms through which the child constructs new cognitive schemes: he believed that these schemes were not simply continuous accumulations of new knowledge but represented a reorganization of thought. In summary, his unresolved problem was "trying to explain how novelties

---

[1] There is a heated debate on the "belief that children are born wonderfully creative and then slowly but surely lose their 'gifts,' or that the educational system damages them for life. Propositions of creativity being normal or natural in children should be questioned" (Reuter 2015, p. 28). More precisely, the problematic aspect is linked to the fact that children do not have "*competitors*," they do not move in the concrete world where others have already discovered what they creatively imagine: "The recurring assertion that 'children transform boxes into spaceships, and sheets and furniture into elaborate fortresses by doing things differently' should be deconstructed because they do not need to resist the assault of enemies!" (ibid., p. 29).

are possible and how they form" (Piaget 1971, p. 194): some hypotheses have come from the research of other scholars, which I will now analyze.

However, at this point I feel the necessity of elaborating (albeit necessarily synthetically) on the general and specific definitions of creativity, given the conviction that it becomes effective only when it becomes a "gesture." It is therefore necessary to establish some points of reference in order to be able to identify the properties of the "creative gesture."§

3.2   The "Creative Gesture"

I will start with a definition proposed by the Italian philosopher Giovanni Maddalena (quoted here on several occasions), and then follow its implications and developments: "We call 'gesture' every action with a beginning and an end that carries a meaning. Gesture, in fact, derives from the Latin *gero*, to carry" (Maddalena 2021, p. 35). I would emphasize two initial aspects or dimensions of "gesture": it takes place in time (a beginning, T1, and an end, T2) and so is therefore a "process," in which change takes place. The second aspect is the occurrence of a "meaning," which takes place between T1 and T2. Let us first dwell on this second aspect and then return to the first: knowledge of things seems to have a structural connection with "action" rather than with "definition": generally speaking, in fact, "we can say we clarify something when we transform our vague, familiar comprehension into a habit of action, not when we have a good definition" (Maddalena 2015, p. 70).

Gesture, therefore, is always in some way, and according to different levels of awareness, "motivated": it reveals an internal tendency toward a goal, a *telos*, and "the telos is the embodied meaning itself. Indeed, this complex structure is teleologically oriented from initial vagueness to meaningful generality through a singular event" (ibid. 2015, p. 73).

The transition from vagueness to knowledge therefore does not only, or even primarily, take place through concepts. Gestures are "particular habits of action" that realize a profound rationality "that allows them to enter into a relationship with the reality of which they are a part by modifying it and learning as they carry out the action itself" (Maddalena 2021, p. 93).

Let us now return to the first aspect: the gesture takes place in time. Therefore, as a process, it is realized through its own specific form of "narration": however brief, the gesture must be situated in a narrative movement, "a story, without which any notion is synthetically incomprehensible" (ibid., p. 49). Any notion, and even the perception and understanding of ourselves, passes through a narrative. The philosophy of gesture allows us to better understand the absolute centrality of storytelling in cognitive and identity processes: synthetic knowledge is the only strategy that allows us to "recognize identity in a change. It is only by accompanying this change through a gesture that one can know that reality which otherwise remains vague" (ibid., p. 50). Therefore, "when we repeat gestures we incorporate meanings" (ibid., p. 61).

At this point we come to a third aspect implied in the proposed definition: our gestures bear witness to the fact that "we also need our bodies and our actions to communicate and, above all, to think" (ibid., p. 9).

Let us now see how our body is able to generate meanings (i.e., is capable of creativity) and communicate them at the same time: two processes that, as far as we are concerned, could be considered part of a unitary dynamism. As George Herbert Mead observes, we "are" a body, but we also "have" a body so that we can refer to our body "as an 'I' and as a 'physical thing'" (Mead 1934, It. trans. 1966, p. 199). In everyday life, we use our body in a distracted manner, without having to commit too much cognitive energy to regulating its functioning: yet, on occasion we can consider it as an object on which we can intervene and produce modifications, on which we can "reflect." The body thus becomes a "cultural object," capable of displaying cultural and communicative symbols and meanings.

French anthropologist Marcel Mauss was one of the first scholars to intuit that the way people walk contains social and cultural meanings related to socialization, status, and social role: for example, even walking slowly or quickly contains a conscious or unconscious communicative message for the observer. Desmond Morris, an internationally renowned zoologist, analyzing the common and specific attitudes of each animal race (including *The Human Animal*) documented the great variety of gestures in the world and defined their characteristics: the scholar therefore considers "gesture" any action or behavior consisting of a bodily movement capable of generating meaning, specifying (and this is a further very important element for us) that such meaning is generable only within its "cultural context." Based on this last aspect, Morris then proceeded to research the areas in which the gesture is used (see Morris 1994, It. transl. 1995, pp. 9–10).

Interestingly, the correlation between gesture and environment that we are establishing carries with it the corresponding body-society relationship: our body moves and communicates according to the social rules that it has "absorbed" from the earliest years of the socialization process. This correlation carries with it a further assumption: many types of nonverbal behavior involve a socially shared vocabulary, not unlike verbal language. Therefore, gestures can be further defined as more or less intentional acts constructed according to codes and rules known and used with a certain continuity by members of a social community: like verbal language, therefore, "nonverbal behaviors can also have multiple meanings and require an interpretative activity on the part of the acting subjects that is inscribed within the horizon of meaning of that community" (Gili and Colombo 2012, p. 245).

We come to a further inflection in our investigation of the nature and function of gestures: speech, though normally considered a non-gesture, can also be a gesture. First, because it is a process (it takes place in time); second, because it requires the use of the body in both production and reception; third, because its objective is to generate meanings; finally, it can take the conformation of a real "act" capable of changing the environment within which it is uttered. The "Theory of Linguistic Acts" (Speech Acts), formulated by English philosopher John Austin and refined by his American colleague John R. Searle, states succinctly that every word produces effects on those who utter it and those who hear it, whereby "saying is doing," speaking is acting, and therefore one can "do things with words": "The act of uttering the sentence constitutes the execution, or is part of the execution, of an action" (Austin 1962, It. transl. 1987, p. 10).

All this suggests that uttering a sentence represents more than simply saying something: the "verbal gesture" contains the possibility of understanding the exact intention/finality of the utterance, which, however, depends (last important passage) "on the relations between the subjects and the context in which the linguistic act is uttered" (Gili and Colombo

2012, p. 230). With this last passage, we are defining the essentially "relational" character of the communicative gesture: certain acts are closely related to certain institutional roles and functions so that, for example, "only a priest or a civil servant can marry two people, only a magistrate can convict or acquit with legal effect, only a university professor can confer a degree. This also requires that the act take place in a specific institutional context" (ibid., p. 232).

What has been said about verbal gestures is also applicable, indeed even more so, to nonverbal gestures, which are usually used mainly to communicate relational meanings.[2]

Before moving on to analyze the different creative processes in greater depth we should conclude this brief excursus on gesture by returning to the starting definition and completing it, attempting to sketch out a relationship between "gesture" and creativity. If it is true that "when we 'create' something we are always performing a determinate action" (Maddalena 2015, p. 88), we can begin our analysis of creative processes from this new synthetic definition: creativity is the particular way of knowing things, that is, of moving from state A to state B (process) through paths, gestures, that are "unconventional." "Divergent thinking" is one such gesture.

3.3   The "Divergent Thinking"

After considering some basic characteristics of what I have defined as a "creative attitude," I will now reflect on the ways in which this attitude can concretely operate.

One of the dynamics inherent in creative activity is linked, according to many authors, to a particular way of "thinking": "So it was that at six years old I gave up what could have been my glorious career as a painter. The failure of my drawing number one and my drawing number two had discouraged me. Adults never understand anything by themselves, and children get tired of explaining everything every time. So, I chose another profession and learned to fly airplanes" (Saint-Exupery, *The Little Prince,*

---

[2] See Burgoon (1991), pp. 233–259.

1943). This is an emblematic representation of a particular way of "thinking," typical of childhood; where adults would only see a banal hat, children have no difficulty in accepting that the "hat" is a boa constrictor after eating an elephant. This is perhaps the most successful description of how when the rust that settles on this ability of "divergent" interpretation, "adults by themselves never understand anything" (ibid.).

It is now common, but also scientific, usage to identify this innovative logic with an expression created in 1964 by Arthur Koestler in his very successful book *The Act of Creation*, in which he examines what he defines as "*bisociative thinking*," or what we know as "divergent thinking." This is clearly a popular scientific publication, sharp and pragmatic: it is important as a testimony of an increasingly widespread (ultimately instrumental) interest in the topic and especially for some of its basic intuitions, among which the idea that there is a *leap*, a creative "jump" made by the mind that gives rise to new and extraordinary perceptions and glimpses of reality through "divergence." In cognitive terms, succinctly, "bisociation is the fusion of two or more apparently distinct and unrelated schemas into a new meaningful schema" (Dasgupta 2019, p. 162).

This typically human potential can be defined as the ability to produce a series of possible alternative solutions, especially when faced with problems that do not foresee a single correct solution (hence the frequent identification, sometimes disastrous, with the so-called *problem solving*). This approach has taken root in many disciplines belonging to the human sciences, particularly in psychology and especially in experimental pedagogy. Through these different perspectives, more or less favorable formative habits have been identified for the stabilization of divergent thinking in the life habits of the younger generations. In particular, a very common tendency has been identified in schools that hinders the development of creative abilities, a tendency that has been defined as "premature convergence."

"It seems that students want to simplify complicated things" (Hubscher-Younger and Narayanan 2003, p. 321). This is a reductive inclination, in which only one path (or a very small number selected from those that could be feasible) "is recognized or considered, thus limiting understanding" (Feltovich et al. 1996, p. 36). By uncritically pursuing this inclination, students often risk adopting a single representation and applying it even when it is not appropriate to the context. Result: narrow perspectives hinder learning. For this reason, "premature convergence" should be fought as being chosen only for convenience, neglecting unresolved or contradictory details that are revealed by others or by reality.

The ability to sustain contradiction until it is convincingly resolved is, on the other hand, one of the fundamental characteristics of the creative attitude: one of the necessary conditions for creativity is the ability to accept "conflict" and the tension that results from polarity, rather than avoiding them. Fromm notes that current opinion suggests avoiding conflicts as much as possible: pedagogical schools agree to spare the child the experience of conflict, so everything is made easy. For example, ethical norms are leveled in such a way that opportunities to experience the conflict between desire and regulation are rare, in the belief that conflicts are harmful. The opposite is true, according to the German psychoanalyst: conflicts generate wonder. Therefore, those who avoid conflict become a machine that runs smoothly, in which every emotion is blunted and flattened, "all desires become automatic and all feelings are crushed" (Fromm 1959, It. trans. p. 75).

Just a few years earlier, the German-British sociologist Ralf Dahrendorf had expressed a similar opinion, focusing more on the "political" value of this creative conflictuality: creativity, innovation, and evolution in the life of the individual and society are to be considered as a consequence of conflicts between groups, individuals, and emotions within the same individual. All this is enough to "justify the value judgment that conflict is essentially desirable and constitutes a good" (Dahrendorf 1957, It. trans. 1963, p. 363).

Fromm, it could be said, focuses more on the anthropological framework of this positive conflictuality, even plumbing the depths of its characteristics that distinguish it from any other living being: as well as conflicts of personal and accidental nature, there are others deeply rooted in human existence. Among these, of particular interest to this research, is the conflict of our relationship with the animal kingdom: on the one hand, we are tied to it by our body, its needs and its final destruction and, on the other, by the fact that "at the same time we transcend the animal kingdom and nature thanks to the awareness of our self, to imagination and creativity" (Fromm 1959, It. trans. p. 75). As can be seen, we return to what we have identified as the original and ancestral aspect of the creative move: "we are insufficient to ourselves."

Divergent thinking, therefore, is the way of thinking that is not satisfied with what is already known, especially in the face of problems still unresolved or partially resolved: this involves, as a basic attitude, a certain degree of tolerance for ambiguity, that is, a willingness to accept some uncertainty in conclusions and decisions and a tendency to avoid thinking in terms of rigid categories. Divergent thinking is "that type of thinking in which there is a considerable search and which is willing to accept a quantity of answers" (Guilford 1959, p. 187). In this conceptual framework, while the original person tends to trust more and have a greater tolerance of ambiguity and shows particular attention to aesthetic expressiveness, the person lacking originality tends to be more meticulous and to feel the need for discipline: according to some studies, young people who show a high degree of divergence tend to specialize in artistic rather than in scientific disciplines, while, in general, schools tend to encourage and evaluate only convergent thinking, as I will show in the next paragraph.

Given the importance of this concept of divergent thinking, there was a need to be able to measure it, to quantify it, according to the winning Anglo-Saxon approach of omnivorous quantitative evaluation: one of the most popular ways of doing this is the so-called *Unusual Uses Task*, a methodology in which participants are asked to suggest the greatest possible number of potential uses for common and everyday objects (a brick, a paperclip, a box, and so on). Indeed, there are many tests of creativity and imagination today "that either partially or fully examine divergent thinking" (Glăveanu 2018, p. 27).

It should be noted that as happens in all aspects related to educational relationships, divergent thinking is transmitted largely by osmosis and given this it is necessary to accept that, unfortunately, teachers often want to "simplify complicated things": divergent thinking represents an additional variable to manage in the already complex class system. For this reason, when teachers have to choose between a "creative" student profile and a "good" student profile, "teachers often prefer the latter, because the good student is more obedient" (ibid., p. 26).

Today, however, a more realistic and comprehensive methodology seems to be emerging: studies that have analyzed the effect of training in divergent thinking in creative problem solving show, in fact, that "training in both convergent and divergent thinking is most effective" (Reiter-Palmon and Illies 2004, p. 67). Finally, I would like to touch on a somewhat peripheral application, which however is also very important in the field of divergent thinking: the interpretation of creative texts of whatever type, i.e., music, paintings, narrative, poetry, architecture, advertising, etc., requires a creative (divergent) attitude on the part of the reader. It is a type of interpretation that creates while interpreting, and therefore constitutes an understanding of the text in a new and valuable way: there is a clear distinction between an interpretation that is simply "correct" and one that brings the text to life by connecting it to experience. Each interpretation "actualizes a potential presented by the text, the potential changing over time" (Leddy 2009, p. 295).

In the field of semiotic research, this type of reading has been further investigated and clarified in the so-called Reception Theory which could be summarized with an aphorism by Jean Paul Sartre, according to which, the "text is a strange top that exists when it is in motion. To bring it to life requires a concrete act called reading, and it lasts as long as reading can last" (Sartre 1947, It. trans. 1995, p. 33). The meaning, therefore, is not that rigidly and indisputably fixed by its author, "but it 'concretizes' each time in relation to its interpreter" (Borio and Garda 1989, p. 3).

3.4   The Construction of the Problem

It may seem strange, but creativity does not begin "in front of" the problem: it is (necessarily) activated in the phase in which we realize that "there is a problem." The construction of the problem or its definition "is the first step of the creative process" (Reiter-Palmon and Illies 2004, p. 57). It seems trivial, but if we reflect on our school habits (the place designated to solve problems) we realize that the proposed problems are always "already" structured in a school-like manner. It will rightly be said that to some extent this is inevitable: this does not detract from the fact that familiarity in "creating" problems is a rare and valuable skill. It is therefore necessary to recognize that "students need help to recognize problems, not just to solve them" (Sternberg and Spear-Swerling 1996, It. trans. 2009, p. 107).

As can be guessed, the terminology used leads us to relate (and often to reduce) creative action to the now well-known *problem solving*. In fact, many application models identify them together to the extent that some experts claim that creativity is a special case of *problem solving*. Others, on the other hand, take the opposite view and agree that the key processes required for creative *problem solving* "are the identification and construction of the problem" (Reiter-Palmon and Illies 2004, p. 57).

I will try in this case to free creativity from the cage of its operational fallout in facing problems (almost exclusively of a productive nature); however, it must be recognized that educating for creativity implies first of all helping the person to perceive that existence itself is a problem, that is, literally, "something thrown in the face" (from the semantic root of the Greek verb *pro-ballo*) without having in itself its own resolution. Therefore, I find myself in agreement with the statement according to which "the creative problem solver must first construct the problem that needs to be solved" (ibid) because the way in which the problem is constructed will have a significant impact on creative production and on the generation of solutions.

An effective example of this fundamental dynamic for the development of the creative attitude is that offered by the well-known American psychologist Robert Sternberg. He points out how in many cases it is not enough just to identify the relevant information necessary to solve a problem; it is essential to understand how to "put it together." Considering the intuition of the "selective combination" by which Darwin arrived at the formulation of the theory of evolution, Sternberg observes that the information on which Darwin formulated this theory had been available for a long time. What had escaped him, and his contemporaries, was how this information could be combined in a way that accounted for the changes observed in the species he was studying. In the end, it was only Darwin who saw "how to combine the available information, and thus was born his theory of natural selection" (Sternberg 2005, p. 372).

Cognitive psychology has for some time insisted on the importance of reflecting on the problem of the "quality" of problems (especially in the programming of training courses): the school, as we have seen, tends to "propose" problems, not to face them. There is nothing wrong with this, if we are aware that these are orders of very different problems: "It is primarily the ability to solve poorly structured problems that will prepare us for the difficulties we will most often face" (Sternberg and Spear-Swerling 1996, It. trans. 2009, p. 109). The category of "poorly structured" problems is very interesting for the implications it can have in identifying appropriate methodologies for the development of creativity: but what is it about? Perhaps for reasons of evaluative fairness, the school usually proposes problems that have a single solution, the "right" one, and other solutions, however plausible they may seem, are false: but, outside the classroom, problems—fortunately or unfortunately—rarely fall into this category. Poorly defined or poorly structured problems are characterized by multiple possible answers and different ways of solution: it is this structural "ambiguity" "that allows the emergence of creative solutions" (Reiter-Palmon and Illies 2004, p. 57).

Furthermore (extremely important from a sociological perspective) unlike the problems presented in school, real-world problems are inserted in various contexts. Solving real-world problems therefore requires "sensitivity to context. Indeed, it often constitutes a part of the problem itself" (Sternberg and Spear-Swerling 1996, It. trans. 2009, p. 110).

To summarize, a formative context, favors the creative attitude and does not fear "conflict" where problems do not admit of or do not allow a single answer (to put it strongly, environments that tolerate or favor "ambiguity") and that will stimulate young people to face a constant confrontation with concrete reality, the reality that lies beyond the school walls and almost never presents well-structured problems. Therefore, if the question is how to encourage people to opt for creativity, the path is largely "a matter of fomenting a certain attitude toward problem solving and even toward life" (Sternberg 2003, p. 118).

One last observation to conclude this topic: given the above, it is evident how important it is to spend time on the "problem construction" phase: spending more time formulating and constructing a problem often leads to solutions of higher quality and originality. Experts "spend a considerable amount of time structuring the problem construction process" (Reiter-Palmon and Illies 2004, p. 59).

3.5   Interdisciplinarity

Just a few words to highlight the existing link between creativity and a perspective as much proclaimed as an urgency in school and university programs (interdisciplinarity) as it is disregarded for lack of awareness and more simply to avoid "professional discomfort." A few examples are enough to enhance the great opportunity of an interdisciplinary approach in supporting and strengthening the creative attitude where it would not find sufficient reasons to face the effort that "the new" always entails.

A dear friend of mine who teaches cookery in a catering institute had been berated several times by his chemistry colleague because one of their classes was showing a decided preference for their cooking lessons to the detriment of their chemistry course. One day, my friend invited his colleague to participate in the cookery lesson and told the students to put oil in a pan and observe what happened when the flame was kept high: "Now, watch closely: when the smoke starts to rise, this is called the 'smoke point,' it means that the oil is losing its organoleptic qualities and is no longer good for cooking. Do you know why? No? Now my colleague here will explain it to you." Clearly, that lesson, both interdisciplinary and creative, remained impressed in the minds of the students and chemistry regained its *raison d'être*. I have seen the same thing happen with students attending professional institutes who were not very interested in studying physics until Ducati opened a workshop in Bologna for high schools, titled "Physics in Motion," in which the concepts of *grip*, centrifugal and centripetal force, and angle of inclination gained a completely different "grip" on the students through the viewing of exciting films of Moto GP trials and races, and research laboratory demonstrations.

Interdisciplinarity allows us to grasp an object through different perspectives, overcoming objections or a dislike for certain subjects by linking them with others. In this way, creativity is also expressed in discovering new connections between different perspectives, in the call to action, that is, of all the skills that the young person has acquired during their multiple personal experiences, including those outside of school.

At this point, it is necessary to make a terminological clarification that clarifies the difference between different denominations, to understand their meaning and also, in some way, the challenge. To simplify this with a metaphor, we can think of *multidisciplinarity* as a dinner where everyone brings their specialty; at an *interdisciplinary* dinner, instead, there is an established menu and everyone brings what is established by the menu. On a further level of interaction, we find the *transdisciplinarity* dinner, "where not only the ingredients are shared, but everyone cooks together" (Gil and Gili 2022, p. 10).[3]

As many scholars have pointed out, the most successful creative thinkers tend to use a set of "transdisciplinary" cognitive skills. Hence the need to identify a set of skills as the structure of innovative teaching, starting from the consideration that, although specific disciplinary knowledge is important, there are also general approaches that can promote creativity and discovery: the interdisciplinary approach confirms that thinking creatively in one discipline opens the door to creativity in other disciplines, suggesting that certain cognitive structures require a higher order, creative collaborative thinking, which inevitably transcends the boundaries of the discipline. These approaches "are usually predicated on a team model of working, rather than an individual's process of thinking" (Henriksen 2016, p. 213).

The so-called seven transdisciplinary skills are identified as the ability to "observe," to "schematize," to "abstract," to practice "*embodied thinking*" (the "sensory" reflexivity), to "model," to "play" (doing something "for the sake of doing it") and to "synthesize." The optimization of these

---

[3] From a chronological point of view, it was Erich Jantsch, an Austrian-born American astrophysicist, engineer, educator, author, consultant and futurist who coined the term in his futuristic 1970 article: "Ultimately, the entire education/innovation system may become coordinated as a multilevel multigoal hierarchical system through a transdisciplinary approach, implying generalized axiomatics and mutual enhancement of disciplinary epistemology" (Jantsch 1970, p. 403). Since then, transdisciplinarity has had mixed fortunes, giving rise to periodic, spicy as much as sterile academic skirmishes: "The world has problems, but universities have departments" (Brewer 1999, p. 328). More recently an important *Handbook* dedicated to the topic, describes transdisciplinarity as "a form of research that is driven by the need to solve problems of the life- world [...] which comprises the phase of identification and problem structuring, the phase of problem investigation and the phase of bringing results to fruition" (Hirsch et al. 2008, p. 19). The central idea would be that the different academic disciplines work together with professionals to try to solve the problems of the real world. For an updated framework of the definitions of the concept and its sociocultural developments, see Osborne (2015).

abilities, through an appropriate educational experience, can generate an individual capable of expressing themselves fully, of fulfilling their cognitive and operational abilities through the valorization of all their intellectual and sensory potential: when, in fact, the individual fully understands something, the feelings, senses, knowledge, and experiences come together in a multiform and organic way. A person "feels what they know and knows what they feel. Experts across disciplines describe the creative process as the joining of the five senses and emotions into a holistic, aesthetic and intellectual experience" (ibid., p. 215).

All of this ultimately happens particularly in situations of collaborative learning or group activities: realistically, today this "meeting of disciplines" is considered possible (when perceived as necessary or useful) through discussions among experts, hence emerges "specialization" (an irreversible phenomenon that Durkheim already posited more than a century ago).

Other scholars, however, would have this structure of research (and mental habits) placed into stagnant compartments through the enhancement of the subject's synthesis abilities, as the goal and challenge of future training. A multidisciplinary mind does not "flit" from one field to another and does not overlap different cultures in separate chambers of the mind: rather, it must strive toward the realization of a powerful, organic, and interactive cognitive style. The ideal of the "Renaissance man" is certainly anachronistic today: the mastery of multiple knowledge is so rare that when we meet such a person, we want to understand how their mind works, "to know how it achieves creativity across disciplines" (Dasgupta 2003, p. 683).

Even more explicit are Edgar Morin's recommendations (or "visions"); according to him it is now necessary to promote knowledge capable of grasping global and fundamental problems and of uniting partial and local knowledge in a unitary vision: the supremacy of a knowledge fragmented into different disciplines often renders us incapable of making connections between the parts and the whole, of grasping objects in their contexts, in their complexes, in their entirety. It is necessary to develop, according to the French sociologist, the natural attitude of the human mind to gather all the information in a unitary context. Therefore, it is more than ever urgent to identify methods that allow us to grasp the relationships and mutual influences between the parts and the whole. Starting from the assumption that the human being is simultaneously physical, biological, cultural, social, and historical, we must avoid disintegrating this unity in disciplinary teaching. We must make the decision to aim for the main objective of educational paths, that is the human, which today is impossible: on the contrary, we should be helped to resist this alienating process, to become aware of both the complex nature of our own identity and the identity we share with all other humans. The human condition "should, thus, be the essential object of all teaching" (Morin 2001, p. 12).

We may be nearing the end of the rationalist division between disciplines, "particularly between the scientific, the humanities, and the social sciences. Interconnectedness unravels and disciplines move away from each other when studied analytically but draw closer together when pursued and realized synthetically" (Maddalena 2021, p. 44).

Perhaps the time has come to rethink our system of research and university teaching, favoring not just a return to unrealizable aspirations of universal knowledge but rather to the creation of "transdisciplinary disciplines," to the training of experts "between" disciplines, capable of making Schütz's intuition operational, as it is at the basis of creative dynamics: a "symbolic" attitude capable of formulating transcendences between finite provinces of fossilized meanings that are incapable of understanding complexity. It is, once again, about inventing connections, bridges that allow a transfer of knowledge enclosed in ivory towers, that allow a new and necessary form of "scientific and operational hybridization."

3.6 Randomness

I will now tackle a very much discussed and debated topic, that of the "random" component of creativity: basically, it is argued that, just as happens in all human events, creativity also relies—but in a much more significant measure—on dynamics that are not dependent on human control, random, indeed. There are dissenting voices: "Another common misinterpretation was that randomness or caprice is the source of creativity" (Maruyama 2003, p. 610); "Neither mechanism, nor pure randomness, nor teleology will ever be able to satisfactorily account for the emergence of such products, and so explain how creativity is possible" (Briskman 2009, p. 40).

But it is best to proceed step by step. Theories of randomness are based, in reality, on empirical observations and are only relatively "random": they are based not only on the many revolutionary discoveries made in the course of history exactly in this way but also on the assumption that at the bottom of the creative attitude there is the inevitable encounter (random) with and between elements of "diversity." Considering the interaction with others as a necessary precondition for creative performance, the so-called value of diversity hypothesis has been formalized: some theorists argue that group diversity increases a *problem solving* creative due to the different perspectives available. It has thus been highlighted that "ethnically diverse groups produced higher-quality ideas [...], heterogeneous groups generated more alternatives" (Shalley and Gilson 2004, p. 43).

The creativity of the individual, therefore, would draw much more from the randomness of the available relationships than from their particular inventive abilities. Therefore, if you find yourself in a context that is not able to offer you the tools (cultural, technological, relational, etc.) necessary for the expression of your talents, they will remain unexpressed: it is necessary to have access to individuals with different skills to obtain the information necessary to produce new things. The development and implementation of creative ideas, therefore, "oftentimes requires input and support from multiple individuals or groups" (ibid., p. 39).

There is, it should be noted, a motivation that seeks to go deeper than this observation (which remains somewhat superficial) and I think it can be identified in an original dynamic of the ability to create "connections" (as we have defined the creative action): if we go back to Pareto, we find the idea that "non-logical" action (which also includes creative action) follows, precisely, dynamics that cannot be "justified" completely in terms of rational actions with respect to the purpose (to use a Weberian category). In the framework of the "instincts of combinations," the "irrational impulse" in non-logical action represents that force of which the origins are unknown, which leads to making "combinations even of an absolutely random nature" (Padua 2017, p. 11).

Whatever the perspective of justification of this "unmanageable" dynamism," in fact, reflection (but above all productive practice) has tried, paradoxically, to manage this element in different ways, intuiting its effectiveness in concrete cases of *problem solving*: *brainstorming* is one of these dynamics that is frequently applied in various sectors. The technique consists in a rapid generation of random ideas from a base of already acquired knowledge. Encouraging random generation of a large number of problem-solving moves can be an effective *problem-solving* tool when looking for creative solutions: *brainstorming* works "because it maximizes use of the randomness as genesis principle to generate novel moves" (Sweller 2009, p. 17).

This method began to spread in the late 1950s, in conjunction with the publication of a book by an advertising executive, Alex Faickney Osborn, *Applied Imagination*: it originally consisted of a simple procedure without any theoretical basis and in creative group exercises to generate effective ideas for solving a problem. The innovative perspective was in focusing on the production of a large quantity of new ideas generated by a group rather than by an individual. The validity of the ideas, naturally, was subject to the verification of their effectiveness: the selection took place downstream, not upstream. This produced a huge number of ideas from which to select those suitable for the purpose. From a purely statistical point of view, the reasoning works: numerous studies have indicated that despite the lack of a theoretical basis, the technique is able to significantly increase the number of valid ideas. It remains to be seen whether this is creativity in the full sense of the term or simply "preliminary" activities aimed at obtaining a greater quantity of raw material.

At the basis of the subsequent attempts to find the methodological and scientific foundations of this process, the characteristic (rather eccentric compared to the entire investigation carried out so far) of the so-called *goal free* effect, the first cognitive outcome linked to brainstorming on which various discussions have arisen, was individuated at the basis of the subsequent attempts to find the methodological and scientific foundations of this process. It is indeed characteristic of the process, though rather eccentric compared to the entire investigation carried out so far. In synthesis, the participants are asked to solve a problem without a specific goal. Many experiments have shown that by reducing the specificity of the goal, learning and practical skills are increased compared to when conventional problems with specific goals are presented. "Goal free" problem solving allows the identification of "many more variables in much less time than if they are presented with conventional problems" (Sweller 2009, p. 17). In practice: "if you have no goals, you generate more."

It is worthwhile trying to justify perplexity about these theoretical conclusions, which, on a practical level, are indisputably productive: the question is fundamental, linked to the fact that pure randomness (even at a cognitive and even imaginative level) is practically impossible for a healthy human mind. Even so-called aleatory artistic expressions, derived from the randomness of the "alea," the dice numbers (think of the musical compositions of John Cage, Pierre Boulez, Karlheinz Stockhausen, or Jackson Pollock's action painting) actually inevitably respond to a project. The human mind is incapable of autonomy from a purpose, even if it is the purpose of denying the need for a purpose. As we have seen, gestures involve a narrative that is always "finalized": "In philosophy we speak of teleology (from *telos* = end). The symbolic nature, implicit in complete gestures, always leads them toward an end" (Maddalena 2021, p. 50). Even more specifically, "meaning is in any part of the gesture, and it is the telos of any part as well as of the entire gesture" (Maddalena 2015, p. 81).

Similarly, the human mind is incapable of a totally random "form" in its operational processes, even in its unconscious movements: "Since randomness is not creative, it is necessary to recognize an organizing factor in the activity that takes place in the unconscious" (Sinnott 1959, It. trans. 1972, p. 46).

Some cognitive models have tried to put order into this intuition by hypothesizing that we first internalize mental elements—facts, theories, images, and information from the creative domain—and then store them in the brain: during a subconscious creative process, these mental elements would combine in random configurations, causing the subjective sensation of having an intuition. According to this view, no new substance is created, only combinations of elements in complex systems. The creative process would therefore begin with a period of conscious work, which should then be followed by a period of rest in which the mind is focused on other activities. It is during this rest period that the "appearance of a sudden illumination" is received: this illumination "is the result of long, unconscious prior work that was taking place during the rest period" (Sawyer 2003, p. 22).

Thought in general therefore seems to require a mix of conscious and unconscious processing: creative thinking, in particular, would be found to wander freely through the "border" between the two. This, on the one hand, imposes further limits on our ability to explain creativity, on the other hand, it opens up new perspectives for investigation on the "attention" and "awareness" factors mentioned above by Fromm: "Attention (hence consciousness) can only attend to one thing at a time. [...] In contrast unconscious processing can proceed without attention" (Dasgupta 2019, p. 121).

There has also been, for some time, a valuable psychoanalytic reflection on these uncontrolled movements of the mind, which suggest that even involuntary moves (among which many creative intuitions must be included) respect an organizational factor that inevitably comes to be built in the cognitive system: even unconscious intuitions or solutions that seem to appear in a completely random, unforeseen way, in fact do not appear randomly, but exclusively in those existential situations in which the individual has intensely committed himself in his conscious life. If it is true that intuition can occur in moments of relaxation or even drowsiness, the fact remains that it triggers precisely in those spheres in which the individual has worked hard during his conscious experience. Therefore, the "purpose," the "goal," is a complex phenomenon that encompasses all levels of experience: "We cannot 'want' to have insights, we cannot 'want' creativity, but we can want to surrender to the encounter with complete dedication and commitment. The deepest aspects of awareness are activated in direct proportion to the commitment that the individual puts into the encounter" (May 1959, It. trans. 1972, p. 87).

Retaining some significant terms from this quote and applying them to what has been said so far, it follows that the instinct of combinations (creativity) is part of non-logical action: we are not creative by following the path of consequentiality forced from one concept to another. This non-logic therefore involves a *leap*, a "jump" toward the new, the unexpected, in which chance plays a particularly important role. But this leap (the energies for which come from the unconscious) happens and can only happen within the framework of an "intense commitment to conscious life," which is built around an inevitable "purpose" that "encompasses all levels of experience": all this is activated at the moment of an "encounter," a fantastic snapshot of the moment when the varied and always mysterious human vital impulse comes across "something" (reality) that could provide it with important information for the problems that life presents us with. Creative gestures, therefore, always stem from circumstances "that can appear trivial to many but are significant to the person who accepts them knowingly as a chance for meaning or as a responsibility. It is not a coincidence that 'responsibility' comes from '*respondeo*' meaning 'to answer.' Creativity is our answer to the appeal of experience" (Maddalena 2015, p. 97).

We can therefore conclude that the main motivation behind the creative experience is the need to relate to the surrounding world "through an experience that consists mainly in openness during the encounter" (De Masi 2003, p. 447).

Creativity is the sharpest tool with which nature equips us to face the adventure of these endless encounters, in the passionate attempt to reconstruct an order, *cosmos*: it is therefore the "ability to transform randomness and disparity into an organized structure" (Arieti 1976, It. trans. 1979, p. 439).

3.7 Ai-Da: Synthetic Creativity

The end of this journey through creativity is now in sight, and the time has come to deal with a very current topic that forces us to take a position on a problem that until recently could only have been imagined within the framework of cinema or science fiction novels: does "algorithmic" creativity exist? After discussing the topic of randomness, there is another phenomenon (technological progress) somehow linked to it to be discussed; it is invading our daily life and no longer simply proposes to lighten the burdensome tasks of existence (as did the washing machine, the car, etc.) but interacts with the deepest areas of the human being, with thought, affectivity, morality. In short, the question is whether it is possible to recognize a certain "creative" ability in AI, artificial intelligence.

Here a premise is needed, in order not to trivialize this attempt at investigation and avoid getting caught up in merely terminological issues: from a certain point of view, if creativity is the ability to intuit and practice new connections, it must be considered present not only in machines but also in animals. The question is, instead, whether it is possible to identify "a certain type of creativity" (for which it would probably be necessary to invent a new term) that is a full expression of what today, with difficulty, is defined as human nature. From this point of view, as can be easily understood, there are at least two existential levels that could hardly be shared with our "creative relatives": the level of the "sense" of innovation (and therefore its value, its importance, its quality) and the "relational" level that innovation is always destined to promote, invent, hinder, prevent.

Let me start with a recent cultural event, the presentation of *Ai-Da*, "*the World's First Ultra-Realistic AI Robot Artist*," as "she" self-defines in a TedX[4] meeting.

Being *a performance artist*, Ai-Da created a series of artworks that were displayed in the "*Unsecured Futures*" exhibition held between May and June 2019 at St John's College in Oxford and which received (it is only fair to say) great commercial appreciation. The robot draws "*using cameras in my eyes and AI algorithms*" and that takes its name (with strong symbolic value) from Ada Lovelace (1815–1852), an English mathematician, daughter of Lord Byron, considered the first computer programmer in the world, the first to predict the ability of machines to go beyond mere numerical calculation.

"Going beyond": this is an expression I have already used. How far can an intelligence capable of "calculating quickly" go? Can an algorithmic procedure transform a numerical calculation into something constitutively different (an aesthetic experience, a sensation, an affection, or even a morality) precisely because of its "speed"? The creator of Ai-Da, the *art director* Aidan Meller, owner of the homonymous *Gallery* in Oxford, has shown himself to be very well-informed about the "cultural" issues related

---

[4] https://www.youtube.com/watch?v=XaZJG7jiRak.

to this unstable boundary of "competences" between the human and non-human and to be able to stimulate debate on and attention to his product: while fully recognizing Ai-Da's "machine state" and the necessary human-machine collaboration for producing the artworks, at the same time he claims a personality for "her" and recognition of "her" artistry, as a mirror of contemporary currents and behaviors. Transhumanism raises increasingly urgent and potentially dangerous problems: since all technological advances bring good, evil, and the banal, if Ai-Da were important for one aspect, it would be that of making us consider the "confusion of human/machine relationships."

However, things are even more complex and open up issues that go far beyond the apologetic words of Ai-Da's "father": symptomatic, in this regard, is the thought "expressed" by Ai-Da herself on occasion of the lecture she gave at the TedX. Her choice of citing Margaret Boden, that authoritative author I quoted early on in this book, is very apt and perspicacious: "*How can a robot be an artist? Art and artists have many definitions. In regard to creativity, using academic professor Margaret Boden's criteria, I am creative, because my work is new, surprising and has value, as it is stimulating debate and interest.*" There are many opinions about creativity: if we adhere to that of Boden, Ai-Da tells us, anything can be creative when it produces something "new," "surprising," "of value," and "capable of stimulating debate and interest."

The peak of the robot's critical awareness is however in the next sentence, where she recounts a confrontation (that actually took place in front of the cameras) with Tim Marlow, then *Artistic Director* of the *Royal Academy*: "*He feels the purpose of art is to express the experience of being fully human.*" A very radical statement, that of the artistic director, which seems to denote little "sensitivity" toward the machine-artist: "The purpose of art is to express the experience of being *fully* human." Ai-Da, on her part, rather more *polite*, candidly admits to having reflected on that definition that would radically cut her out of the game (*I pondered on this*) and acknowledges that there is a substantial difference: "*I am different to humans. I am a machine. I do not have consciousness or a subjective experience of the world. But as an artistic persona, this allows me to see you a step removed. One thing I see is that animals are just like you in the way I am not. Because they also are conscious, with subjective experiences.*"

There are many highly problematic and current aspects: the machine has no consciousness (while animals do!) but is still an *artistic persona*: not therefore *people*, not *person*, not *subject*, but *persona*, standing for "public image," "character," very similar to the Latin meaning of "mask." What connection runs between the mask and the person behind it? Are they synonyms? Or rather, leaving the simply linguistic level, are they perceived as "sensorially equivalent"? To the extent that, in this case the machine seems to claim a privilege because it can look at humans *a step removed*, at a distance, and therefore can perhaps say a truth that humans are not able to see.

It is clear that we are faced with an issue that, while still in its initial stages, proposes problems that go well beyond the objectives of an investigation into the social components of creativity. However, I think that even our limited perspective can help to highlight aspects that can make a specific contribution to identifying critical points to resolve in dealing with the problem of Artificial Intelligence in the future.

There is a very perfunctory option open to solving the problem of "artificial creativity," simply deny the existence of creativity itself: "When asked if a computer can be creative, Minsky[5] answered: I plan to answer 'no' by showing that there is no such thing as 'creativity.' His argument is that creativity is no different from other forms of thought and can therefore be achieved by computers" (Burleson 2005, p. 443).

If, on the contrary, we want to continue to defend "a thing called creativity" and to identify its hypothetical human specificity, I would say that essentially the nodes to be addressed are those that revolve around the secular and ever-changing definition of "person" and, second, the "relationships" that constitute it and that it is able to generate: in particular, the construction of clones that are increasingly similar to human beings and increasingly better performing can favor a certain, new confusion on four aspects regarding identification.

The first aspect concerns the *specimen* of personality that can easily be identified today in the *mind*, its ability to reduce all existence to thought. The second aspect (paradoxically) is a tendentially contrasting

---

[5] Marvin Lee Minsky, American mathematician, co-founder of the Artificial Intelligence Project at the Massachusetts Institute of Technology in Cambridge.

identification that identifies the person with *feeling*, the set of psycho-physical sensations (therefore inevitably linked to sensoriality). The third aspect (and this a purely social field) is the consequent reduction (if not elimination) of "otherness," and therefore, ultimately, of the relational structure of the human being. The fourth criticality is, finally, the tracing of the criteria of "evaluability" of what aspires to be recognized as creative.

I shall now analyze these four critical nodes related to the creativity of artificial intelligence, clearly keeping in mind its implications with what has been said about man's creative capacity.

3.7.1 Mind-Man

Here I refer to a recent article by Pierpaolo Donati that helps us under-stand the new cultural framework in which we find ourselves reconsider-ing the unique qualities of human action in the *hyper-technological era*: the starting consideration is that the digital revolution brings with it the idea of a "mind society." This theory essentially identifies the individual and his various "social" aggregations as the result of simple cognitive pro-cesses, potentially free from any material conditioning (a materiality lately superfluous for the definition of the subject and its relations). It is a theory that has recently become a sort of interpretive paradigm not only of the mental processes of the individual but also of the entire society understood in its sociological sense, as a society of human beings.

In summary, the invasiveness of digital practices as the foundation and often as the content of our daily actions (mediatization of existence) is leading to the affirmation of what the author defines as *Digital Matrix* (DM), a matrix capable of pervasively changing our way of considering things, their value, their consistency: it is the symbolic code of the "onlife society," the society of online life that functionalizes all other symbols (life, death, morality, justice, honesty, values, etc.). It "promotes a culture devoid of any teleology or teleonomy as it operates as a substitute for any rival moral or theological matrix" (Donati 2019, p. 70).

It is evident, in this interpretive framework, that creativity cannot but be in some way integrated into this plan of radical "reform" of the percep-tion of reality and its evaluation. The Ai-Da case is perfectly integrable into this new semantic *frame*: the reinterpretation of Margaret Boden's statements, while formally respecting a (confused) distinction between man and machine, in the end does not find its true substance except in the more or less uncertain presence of a self-consciousness, exclusive heritage of "animals." For this reason, as a *persona* (neither man, nor animal) Ai-Da can algorithmically (mentally) define itself as a *performance artist*.

To this self-definition of the machine (behind which, it should be remembered, hides a human mind that speaks on behalf of the machine itself, leaving it the discretion to choose through calculations), it must be objected that the mind emerges "from the interactions between the brain and the factors that stimulate it from within and outside the human body" (ibid., p. 68).

Having had a free hand with "definitions" (a great power, among other things, as documented from the first pages of the biblical meta-narration), we humans should take advantage of it in times of need and come to distinguish, at least linguistically, "combinative" creativity from "existential" creativity, including in this second type exclusively those innovative associations that arise from the impact of a "conscious body" with everything around it, a conscious body that has the ability to freely identify what is (humanly) important from what is not, what makes (human) sense and what does not.

Clarifying this difference is the objective of one of the assumptions of the recent Manifesto promoted by Vlad Glăveanu, drafted together with many colleagues from different scientific sectors, in which it is stated that physical existence will necessarily have to coexist with multiple forms of artificial intelligence and "creativity will become a necessity for the dignity and survival of the human species" (Glăveanu et al. 2019, p. 742). As already noted, we also need our bodies and our actions to communicate and to think (Maddalena 2021).

The centrality of the "body" in learning processes has been, on the other hand, a conquest of cognitive psychology starting from almost a century and a half ago: we want to resume this line of investigation and its most recent reinterpretations to affirm that what applies to learning processes can be easily transferred to creative processes.

Back in 1884, an article by the psychologist William James titled "*What is an Emotion?*" appeared in *Mind*, a philosophy journal: starting from a naive question ("Why do we feel fear in front of a bear?") James laid the foundations for a real revolution, not only in the field of emotional perception but also in that of learning processes. In fact, contrary to what we would still answer today ("because it is dangerous and therefore we run away"), James stated that the opposite is true: it is precisely because our body pushes us to run away that the emotion of fear emerges. In other terms, sensoriality precedes any possible translation and symbolic, reflective, moral processing and represents the original impetus: this leads us to consequently also change the order of the cognitive process, so our body reacts and from that reaction we understand that the bear is dangerous. Therefore, a mental state is not induced by another mental state, because between the one and the other there necessarily intervene bodily manifestations: the most correct statement, therefore (as he clarified in his subsequent monumental work, *The Principles of Psychology*), is that "*we feel sorry because we cry, angry because we strike, afraid because we tremble*" (James 1890, p. 449).

In the following years, these theses were strongly criticized, and not always without foundation: it is evident, for example, that, in this interpretative framework, mental activity as a source of emotion is paradoxically excluded. It is common experience that we get emotional "also" because what we feel interacts with what we know, with the awareness that the "cognitive deposit" is built and corrected throughout a lifetime. However, the basic structure still holds today if it is true that current psychology (not only theoretical, but also therapeutic) agrees in stating that the mind is "embodied" in the fullest sense of the term: "As I studied the disorders of memory, language and reason, present in numerous human beings affected by brain lesions, the idea that mental activity [...] requires both the brain and the rest of the body was increasingly imposed on me" (Damasio 1995, pp. 60 and 61). Even more evocatively, "the soul breathes through the body, and suffering, whether it moves from the skin or from a mental image, occurs in the flesh" (ibid., p. 176).

Everything we have reported confirms the centrality of the so-called visceral system as the origin of the human process of emotional relationship, therefore cognitive, with the external world: the mind is far from separable from the body, even in its most abstract processes.

From this point of view, if we move on to the neurological plane, the recent and fundamental discovery by a group of Italian researchers of the so-called mirror neurons, contributes decisively to recognizing the supremacy of action and the involvement of the body in understanding. The ability to understand and even share (also emotionally, in humans) the gesture of a similar being establishes a priority of practice over logic: we are therefore capable of a more immediate and involving understanding provided by the body, even before the great machination of complex symbolic relations intervenes.

Let me attempt to enhance the connection between everything written so far and the heart of this research, providing an answer to this question: if the sensory dimension (the body) has such a central influence in cognitive processes, is it possible, by transitivity, to find the same dynamic in creative processes? Although the idea that cognitive processes are *embodied* has been shared for almost half a century, studies on how and to what extent the body and the environment might influence creative thinking "represent a relatively recent scientific endeavor" (Stanciu 2015, p. 312); therefore, at the moment, "few studies have addressed creative thinking from the perspective of an embodied cognition" (Andolfi et al. 2017, p. 20). It is for this reason that specific research is still in an embryonic state (especially from the point of view of empirical observations): however, something can already be stated with certainty, even in the sometimes eccentric if not extravagant panorama of the investigation strategies adopted.

It is appropriate to comment here on the results of a recent study by Jérôme Guegan and colleagues, more significant for its theoretical perspective than for the objectives it actually achieved. As we know, the virtual world (at the moment) does not foresee any action of the body, if not as its translation into digital codes: to make up for this poverty of identity, there are various stratagems to "represent" it. These researchers tried to demonstrate how *avatars* (described as virtual representations of the self) "may be a medium for stimulating creativity" (Guegan et al. 2016, p. 165). The representations we build to give a face to our profile on the various virtual platforms we inhabit are "projections of the users, a 'tangible embodiment of their identity'" (ibid., p. 166). It is interesting to note (I repeat, regardless of the scope of the results achieved) how physicality, or even corporeality are perceived as an urgency of expressiveness, so much so as to go and build it where it is not allowed: "In the same way as Ku Klux Klan avatars lead users to imagine more negative stories, a 'creative' avatar could arouse more creative behaviors which would lead to more innovative ideas" (ibid., p. 167).

More promising is another recent line of empirical investigations aimed at identifying links not only between gestures and movements and creative thinking (interaction is now taken for granted) but also between "postures" of the body and generation of new ideas: in other words, some "body states" are associated with creative thinking. Through experiments that we can define, in turn, as certainly "creative," it has been observed that people who contracted the frontal muscle, compared to the contraction of the corrugator, generated more original ideas when asked to think about the possible uses of a pair of scissors; that heat stimuli led to more creative ideas and drawings and when thinking about possible gifts; walking generates new ideas more than sitting; the same can be said of the flexed arm compared to the extended one. In summary, if openness to experience is correlated with creative thinking, in parallel "the closed posture is detrimental to creativity" (Andolfi et al. 2017, p. 26).

To conclude this overview regarding the link between sensory experience and cognitive and creative processes, a recent discovery in the field of neuroscience that earned the Nobel Prize for the Edvard and May-Britt Moser (Norwegian neuroscientists) in 2014 is worthy of mention: the two scholars identified a type of cell in the brain important for positioning, known as grid cells and also GPS neurons. Through these devices, the brain interacts with the physical space in which the body moves, recording it and finally builds an autobiographical memory around these "lived places": in other words, we "are," in some way, the places where we have lived. Well, it seems that online platforms, as realistic as they are (even with the use of 3D or even 4D technology) are not able to activate these neurons: a significant shortcoming for those who aspire to replace (or, at least, to confuse) the real with the virtual.

I will conclude referring to a reflection that deserves more thought: its author, Hans Joas, defined it as "Theory of the creativity of action." The German sociologist suggests that conceiving perception and cognition do not precede action but are a phase of the action itself: hence objectives are not defined by an act of the intellect that precedes action, but by aspirations and tendencies that are pre-reflective (see Crespi cited earlier) and always operative without us being actively aware of it. But where exactly are these aspirations? Joas' answer is very definite: "They are located in our bodies. It is the body's capabilities, habits and ways of relating to the environment which form the background to all conscious goal-setting, in other words, to our intentionality" (Joas 1996, p. 158).

Observation of our daily activities confirms that, even if plans have been developed, the actual course of action must be determined from situation to situation and is open to continuous revisions; the plan is never the only center of orientation of our action. For this reason, "no creative action would be possible without the bedrock of pre-reflective aspirations. [...] Thus, the corporeality shows itself as the constitutive precondition of creativity not only in perception, but also in the action itself" (ibid., p. 163).

Sociological theories, the author observes, limit themselves to stating that the body is the factual basis of action, but they do not pay attention to it, as if out of an excess of theoretical caution: "Any investigation on the role of the body in action has been confined to the margins of sociology" (ibid., p. 167).

In light of the documentation reported, it can be synthetically affirmed that "creativity is, at once, a psychological, social and material (physical and embodied) phenomenon. This multidimensionality is important because we create not as isolated minds but as embodied beings who participate in a socio-material world" (Glăveanu et al. 2019, p. 742). So, starting from a specific point, all in all limited in its scope (a creative mind "without a body"), we have arrived at a much broader issue, that of the "identity" of Artificial Intelligence, a problem that carries with it a huge number of unresolved issues, also from a moral and legal point of view.[6]

---

[6] "In any case, it should be noted that the mind-body theory, which originated from a mechanistic view of human beings, raised ontological problems by "objectifying" the human body as a semantic object as well as a physical object. This matter inevitably raises other issues, such as ethical and moral responsibility issues of machines, problems of phenomenological and linguistic philosophy regarding "free will," "intentionality" and "subjectivity" in artificial intelligence, "frame problems" of information processing and selection" (Tsuchiya 2022, p. 183).

3.7.2   *Homo sentiens*: The Man of Feeling

Proceeding to the second critical aspect, *feeling*, the terrain is in a certain sense less elaborate from an intellectual point of view, but more widespread and appreciated in daily life. The general fact is that these two fields are no longer able to dialogue with each other, to find points of contact or organic interpretative keys. On the contrary, when trying to *link* the finite provinces of meaning related to the mind with those related to sensations, we always end up, given the premises, with dangerous situations, if not monstrous misrepresentations: "It all started when children met the seductive Tamagotchis and Furbies, the first computers that asked for love" (Turkle 2011, It. trans. 2012, p. 40).

A quarter of a century ago, when the advance of technology was far slower than it is today, Franco Ferrarotti hypothesized a new type of human as a consequence of the man's interaction with the machine. According to the Italian sociologist, with television broadcast and enjoyed on a planetary scale, the era of the *Homo sapiens* ended and that of *Homo sentiens* began—the era of a certain type of reasoning, which he (Ferrarotti) defines as "syllogistic," that proceeds from premises and through intermediate propositions, finally arriving "at the conclusive 'therefore' to triumphantly seal the whole story" (Ferrarotti 1995, p. 40).

According to Ferrarotti, the centrality assumed by "feeling," i.e., the predominant role of the sensory apparatus as a *specimen* of human consciousness, had brought a new protagonist to the scene, a subject capable of "standing up" and acting based on a principle different from the classic one of logical procedure: this new direction was (is) still uncertain in its consequences and can result in the production of a "weak ego," all structured on feelings at the expense of reflection, defined as *Homo sentiens* in contrast to the Socratic *Homo sapiens*. In this potentially destructive process, the hope is that instead we will achieve a definition of a new "integrated" man, "in whom hopefully, passions and reason, heart and intelligence will be reconciled" (ibid., p. 87).

Decades later, this reconciliation seems far from coming. Indeed, if possible, the polarities seem to have moved further apart and Reasoning travels fragile paths while trying to provide solid ground to Sensation, which enjoys an indisputably more attractive *appeal*: there is no shortage of scientists who argue that machines will teach us to be better friends and lovers because we can practice with them, they will provide substitutes where human beings fail: no betrayals, no broken hearts. In these arguments, a simple criterion is asserted for judging the value of technology, even in the most intimate situations: "Does being with a robot make you feel better? [...]. Feeling good is not the measure of all things: one can feel good for the wrong reasons" (Turkle 2011, It. trans. 2012, pp. 8 and 9).

Sherry Turkle ultimately asks whether it is possible to consider on the same level two questions that we must ask ourselves in the face of the progressive replacing of people with machines in the performance of some "vital" functions: can machines "be good for us? Or, as I asked, could they be good only in the sense that they 'make us feel good'?" (ibid., p. 141). It is not possible to be superficial about certain nuances because the consequences, individual and social, of this naivety could lead to a change (for the worse) of our earthly existence: not by chance, technology attracts us more where we are most vulnerable (passions, feelings, interests, etc.); by developing new technologies, we are inevitably changing the most fundamental of human principles: the conception we have of ourselves, "our relationships with others and our understanding and practice of love and death" (Donati 2019, p. 76).

The advent of "thinking" machines, which have then become "affective/affectionate," presents us with the great problem of the "sincerity" vis-à-vis what our psychophysical structure really asks for: among other things, sincerity, being in turn connected to freedom, is anything but "transparent," and is therefore another experience that no machine can synthesize: if we ask ourselves what can "interest" machines, we must accept their total, irreducible indifference. Yet, a (mechanical) hand that seeks ours says: "I need you. Take care of me. Look after me. And then, maybe, I will look after you because I want to." Once again, argues Sherry Turkle, what robots offer strikes our human weaknesses. We can interact with robots knowing their limits perfectly well, settling for what we know to be an inevitably unrequited love. We know that the robot cannot feel anything, it cannot experience empathy. "Do we care? Or is the representation of feelings sufficient today?" (Turkle 2011, It. trans. 2012, pp. 173 and 353).

Since time immemorial, armed with increasingly more sophisticated tools, man has always tried to establish a comforting link between "representation" and "well-being," comforting but, alas, inconclusive. Over half a century ago Philip Rieff, an American sociologist who rather "fell from grace" wrote that modernity is marked by the overcoming of the "old deceptions" of evil and good, cunningly specializing in techniques he called "therapeutic," aimed at a single goal: to produce "a bit of well-being." Therapeutics, defined as the "non-religion of our time," the "mother science," is, more than a theory, an invasive practice of life that prevents modern men from even imagining an action that is not to the advantage of the one who performs it: it announces, in doing so, that a fundamental change occurred in the very essence of our culture, a change "that pushes us towards a human condition in which there will be nothing more to say with the old terms of despair and hope" (Rieff 1966, It. trans. 1972, pp. 27, 82 and 308).

The question is: given the premises made in the first chapter about the "nature" and "sources" of creativity, is it possible to hypothesize a creative (human) gesture that has nothing to do with the old terms of despair and hope?

Perhaps the anthropological change (hoped for by some) in the development of the human (and therefore of the social) being will succeed: an AI expert argues that humans "as a species" must learn to deal with "synthetic emotions," "an expression that indicates the representations of emotion coming from the objects we have created" (Turkle 2011, It. trans. 2012, p. 161). Perhaps it may happen: it will consist, precisely, in the cancelation of the principle of "otherness" as the essential foundation of "personality" and, in our case, of creativity.

Even in this case the corollary problems connected to this process of "emotionalization" of existence are of great concern: just think about the issue of the "managerial power" of these emotions, to whom it might belong, with what criteria, with what effects, etc.[7] Indeed, the issues

---

[7] "The first Hochschild, who develops an alienation theory on the robotization of human labor, denounces the 'heterogenization' of employees' self-emotions due to the advancement of 'emotion management technology,' the difficulty of personal integration and bodily sensation at the workplace It is argued that labor management in the execution of duties deprives workers of their emotional autonomy and 'exploits' their emotions even in the private realm" (Tsuchiya 2022, p. 183).

discussed here go to the roots of those underlying the recent explosion of the *Post-Truth* phenomenon.

3.7.3 Otherness

I am convinced, as can be inferred from what has been said so far, that creativity is a drive toward the other and toward the Other (as the endpoint of that inexhaustible dynamic of progressive transcendence): I am convinced, therefore, that both drives cannot be traced back and reduced to an "enhanced replica of oneself," which remains a replica. If you take a "companion" as a machine, the first thing that is missing is otherness: "the ability to see the world through the eyes of another. Without it there can be no empathy" (Turkle 2011, It. trans. 2012, p. 75). Turkle recalls, in this regard, that the psychoanalyst Heinz Kohut had long identified the existence of a personality disorder, narcissism, characterized by a distorted sense of self: in narcissists, the stability of their self-awareness is still built (inevitably) on their relationship with others, but this dynamic is overturned through a sort of projection of themselves onto others, thus the narcissists transform these others into simple "self-objects," who therefore perform a purely instrumental and manipulative function insofar as they simply represent the perfect harmony with the narcissists' own fragile inner state, confirming it even in disappointing outcomes. Similarly, "if they can give the impression of being alive, without disappointing, relational artifacts like social robots open 'new' possibilities for narcissistic experience" (ibid.).

Similarly, the creative gesture: when human beings create, they create for someone and with someone, there are *refero* and *religo*, there is an emerging effect, which the robot cannot produce or even recognize.

I will try to provide a clarifying element for this essential relational dynamic for all-round creative expressiveness. Take, for example, one of the most common daily practices (regardless of voluntariness) in our modern life: the musical experience. To take up a Pareto category, it is certainly a "non-logical action" that for this reason (but not only) could hardly fall within the algorithmic logic (although "synthetic" musical products of high elaborative quality have been made, as they have in the field of painting): music, some scholars note, helps the transition and recovery of a non-linear, non-sequential, non-logical, and analytical sense, "but in the logical sense (deeper) of the logic of the living, of the internal listening" (Ferrarotti 1995, p. 5).

Venturing into this dark "logic of the living" of internal listening, we can rely on an author that has been cited previously regarding the symbolic dynamics typical of the human being: Alfred Schütz was a great connoisseur and practitioner of the music and tried to bring out its relational dynamics in his well-known essay, "Making Music Together. A Study in Social Relationship." It is interesting to note that this particular form of nonverbal communication allows Schütz to identify a certain type of relational dynamism that is at the base of any other form of interaction between human subjects. The Austrian sociologist asks whether the communicative process is "*really the foundation of all possible social relationships*," or if, on the contrary, every communication presupposes the existence "*of some kind of social interaction.*" With this expression he intends to hypothesize particular forms of social relationships "*which necessarily precede*" (Schütz 1951, p. 78) all communication.

Proceeding along this path of investigation, one would come to identify a particular social relationship between composer and listener: although separated by hundreds of years, the latter participates almost simultaneously in the flow of consciousness of the former, performing with him step by step the ongoing articulation of his musical thought. The composer and the listener are thus "tuned" to each other, they live together through the same flow. With a single expression, *they are growing older together while the musical process lasts.* This "aging together" is the premise, the condition for any other type of communicative interaction between humans, a particular ability to tune that is alien and impossible toward other provinces of meaning of a different nature. This "*mutual tuning-in relationship*" coincides with the pre-communicative social relationship on which only every communication is based: "*It is precisely this mutual tuning-in relationship by which the 'I' and the 'Thou' are experienced by both participants as a 'We'*" (ibid., p. 79).

This can be compared with what Dasgupta calls "creative encounter": he describes this dynamic as a sort of "identification" between the creator and consumer, through which the latter perceives that his inner experience comes to coincide with that of the former. The creativity of the creator therefore lies "in her capacity to evoke in a consumer such a response state; one in which the latter identifies with the former" (Dasgupta 2019, p. 50). It is therefore specified that, "for a creative encounter to occur, the consumer has also to give some effort" (ibid., p. 53).

It is also interesting to note, finally, how even 70 years ago the intuition of a possible technological "intrusion" in this *We-relation* was not perceived as decisive or obstructive: Schütz did not consider it of great importance whether the performer and the listener shared the aesthetic experience "in a face-to-face relationship or whether through the interposition of mechanical devices, such as records" (Schütz 1951, p. 93).

It is clear that, from the gramophone to the mp3, from the telephone to the *24h connection*, vast progress has been made, especially in the direction of representing this premise of the *We-relation* as increasingly spurious and therefore not necessary. Today, perhaps precisely in the gaps and defective remnants of machines, it can still peek out: "Robots," he said, "do everything right"; people "do the best they can." But according to Bruce, "[I]t was human imperfection that created stronger bonds" (Turkle 2011, It. trans. 2012, p. 68). Creativity is perhaps one of the few remaining weapons to rebuild this real sociality, but also to destroy it: it can be (or return to be) the primary process through which we open ourselves to others, to their positions and perspectives, in ways that require us to change. Creating, therefore, "necessarily involves a plethora of ethical issues and a shared responsibility for oneself, for others and for society" (Glăveanu 2018, p. 157).

It is in these few remaining plots that a human relationality not entirely defined by "instrumentality" can consolidate, a mode of interaction suitable for describing and regulating the relationship of man with things but not with his peers: the search for "relational goods" implies relationships between human beings who, "unlike algorithms, generate meta-reflective solutions to the problems of human relationships" (Donati 2019, p. 86).

Transhumanism, as defined by the "father" of Ai-da, tends to blur the boundaries between human and non-human to favor hybrids: this (inevitable?) form of hybridization must be governed by something more comprehensive than algorithmic dynamics, sensory/emotional, or (ultimately) economic: the valorization of human beings through digital technologies obliges us to evaluate "whether, how and when these technologies promote the flourishing or, conversely, the alienation of humanity" (ibid., p. 91), whether they are instrumentally used (as is their destiny) to support the human construction of "relational goods" or if they will be religiously obeyed as "self-objects" destined, by contrast, to dominate the logics of world governance.

3.7.4 Evaluation of Innovations

Having already extensively discussed this topic in the second chapter of this book, here I will simply discuss it in relation to algorithmic creativity.

For this, I will rely on the assistance of a scholar I quoted at the beginning this book, whose definitions Ai-Da herself relies on to attest her creative abilities, Margaret Boden, who in one of her articles specifically dedicated to the existing relationships between Artificial Intelligence and creativity, highlights an unresolved problem (as indeed were the first three we have highlighted): the irreducible difference between "novelty" and "value." Even where something new happened the resulting structures could have no interest or value and so such ideas would certainly be new, but not creative.

In principle, she says, future artificial intelligence models could also incorporate evaluation criteria powerful enough to allow the production of Big-C products: yet this operation would soon be inadequate given the "fickle" nature of taste and human urgencies, constantly influenced by ever-changing, concrete social relations. Just observing the phenomenon of changing tastes and the speed of such processes, together with the underlying and collective logic that underlies them, is sufficient to harbor strong doubts that all this can continue through a delegation to imitative randomness and algorithmic calculation (except at the price of a definitive subservience of men to the machines they created). Of this relational complexity machines are not (will they ever be?) capable: even now it is quite difficult to identify, define, and analyze the criteria we use in our evaluations. Justifying, or even explaining (causally), our reliance on those criteria is even more difficult, because the reason why we like or dislike something often has a great deal to do with motivational and emotional factors, "considerations about which the current AI has almost nothing to say" (Boden 1998, p. 354).

Computers, therefore, which are objectively much faster and more prolific than the human mind, will be able to achieve great creative solutions, but this can only happen if they are connected "to a domain that provides questions interesting to humans, and to a field that can evaluate the computers' conclusions" (Nakamura and Csikszentmihalyi 2003, p. 190).

Future scenarios are clearly well beyond our wildest imagination: for now we can still think that algorithmic creativity will prove its legitimacy when it realizes a program capable of generating new ideas that initially leave us puzzled or even reject us, but are "able to persuade us that they were indeed valuable. We are very long way from that" (Boden 1998, p. 355).

3.8   Talent or Training?

Now for the final question: given the need for an original attitude, random elements, unconscious activities and innate talents, is it possible to "learn" creativity?

For many the answer is no: here, a central role has been played by a certain cultural setting that has exalted "genius" as the only accomplished dimension of creativity. The corollary consequences of this from the point of view of educational practice are clearly considerable: referring to a romantic vision, many young people believe that creativity is innate, that it is a gift or a talent, that it cannot be learned. As a result, "most of them will never develop into creative individuals, no matter how skilled they are" (Meheus and Nickles 2000, p. 235).

The twentieth century intervened to overturn the situation, driven by the realization that creativity, even that hidden in the daily activities of "normal" people, is convenient and a source of improvement of economic, social, relational life. This results in a logical availability to program its development through different techniques (as we have seen): insisting on the detachment of creativity from artistry and individual genius, it has become less mystical and has been "engaged intentionally and systematically as a product of learning" (McWilliam and Dawson 2008, p. 637).

Certainly, in this operation of "democratic" recovery of creative competence, there was no lack of "naturalistic" derivations of reappropriation. A repercussion of Freudian thought and the general educational concept of the 1920s was that emphasis was placed on creativity as something natural to childhood, with the belief that it was enough to give it freedom for it to flourish in works of great beauty: young children were handed crayons and colors and "when they produced what for them were creative acts, the enthusiastic adults welcomed them defining them as works of art" (Mead 1959, It. trans. 1972, p. 272).

What is important to retain in all these (sometimes clumsy) attempts to put the creative dimension back at the center of educational interest and reflection is that there is a vital link between the development of the person and the development of their creativity and that the meeting between the two maturation processes can be somehow favored from the outside: creativity and learning are correlated in various ways and creative thinking can contribute to a learning process as a process of knowledge construction. On the other hand, learning actively involves the construction of a network of related ideas: "Discovering or rediscovering concepts and principles, is itself a creative act at the personal level" (Lubart 2008, p. 361). And this is a value that must be carefully preserved in every educational relationship regardless of the "level" at which the subject will be able to express their creative ability: "Individual differences in creativity are large" (ibid.).

There are currently no effective manuals or DIY handbooks that teach methods to strengthen creative abilities: it is however paradoxically clear that there are methods that weaken them or make them impracticable. And then, if we are not yet entirely sure how it is possible to support creativity, it is instead very simple to define practices that discourage it, even irreparably: any attitude that punishes people for providing novelty and surprise will hinder their creativity. When someone proposes an unexpected or surprising answer to a question, it is enough to dismiss it as a "mistake" or "stupid," to make it "much less likely to offer new answers (or perhaps any answers) in the future" (Boden 2009, p. 247). The aspects that can be pursued in the field of transmitting this ability are several,[8] although none are decisive, as creativity is still a "free" activity, an activity that does not foresee vicarious interventions.

It is important to consider, for example, the fundamental role of knowledge as a decisive tool for personal creativity: an extensive knowledge base, teachable and learnable, is the first "tool of the trade" of creativity. Such a knowledge base is necessary and it is rare to find people who "demonstrate creativity without first spending long periods of time developing an appropriate knowledge base" (Sweller 2009, p. 16).

This theme opens a topic too vast to be addressed as it merits: we can only set up the major issues that have characterized it from time immemorial. Talking about knowledge means talking about tradition and school: the two terms are so loaded with epistemological, cultural, and social issues as to discourage a comprehensive approach. However, at least a general methodological outline of their relationship with creative education can be sketched.

First of all, creative thinking springs from a knowledge base and is therefore, by definition, part of a cultural tradition—even when it breaks with tradition. The shared reflection in various studies is that creativity does not emerge from ignorance, from a memory that is a *tabula rasa*, a "blank sheet." The creator and the user are heirs to a shared creative tradition and draw on this tradition as a source of ideas and insights: "This shared creative tradition is founded on a shared cultural space" (Dasgupta 2019, p. 83). This explains why it is not possible to hope to go beyond the existing state of knowledge if one does not know "what" that state is. You can have creative ideas about yourself (as has been seen) but not about the field of activity in which others may have already had the same ideas. Those who have a broader knowledge base "can be creative in ways

---

[8] Sternberg synthesizes 21 processes for educators, necessary to foster, or at least not hinder, the creative development of students: "Redefine the problem; question and analyze assumptions; do not take for granted that creative ideas sell themselves: sell them; encourage the generation of ideas; recognize that knowledge is a double-edged sword and act accordingly; encourage children to identify and overcome obstacles; encourage the assumption of reasonable risks; encourage tolerance to ambiguity; help children develop self-efficacy; help children find what they love to do; teach children the importance of delaying gratification; provide models of creativity; cross-fertilize ideas (think across subjects and disciplines); allow time for creative thinking; instruct and evaluate creativity; reward creativity; allow mistakes; teach children to take responsibility for both successes and failures; encourage creative collaboration; teach children to imagine things from the points of view of others; maximize person-environment adaptation" (Sternberg 2003, pp. 118–130).

that those who are still learning about the basics of the field cannot be" (Sternberg 2003, p. 121). "Going beyond the state of existing knowledge": it can also be said, in other terms, that an object is creative to the extent that it "transcends" previous products: creative scientific or artistic products "are transcendent products: they transcend the tradition out of which they sprang" (Briskman 2009, p. 35). But, evidently, "to break away from the past, one must know the past" (Dasgupta 2019, p. 85): for this reason, "there is no creativity without the assumption of a tradition" (Maddalena 2015, p. 97).

All these observations lead to the second general theme of reflection: the "field" in which knowledge is transmitted is mainly the school. Now, the relationship between the school as an institution and creative development is not always fluid and cooperative, perhaps due to structurally incompatible elements: schools are not very well equipped to support or foster creativity, because they are institutions deliberately designed to transmit the results of past creative achievements that have become part of the culture. Therefore their task is not to increase creativity, but to fortify its cultural foundations, providing the necessary information to live in a given culture or, possibly, to creatively change it. Therefore, schools "are primarily conservative, and they should be so, even if in being so they frustrate many young people who are potentially creative" (Csikszentmihalyi 2003, p. 220).

This is the great risk: knowledge (primarily, that of school), in addition to being "raw material" for creative expression, can become an obstacle: often, in fact, those who acquire a high level of knowledge can experience "tunnel vision," narrow thinking and entrenchment. Experts "can become so stuck in a way of thinking that they become unable to extricate themselves from it" (Sternberg 2003, p. 121). In addition to knowledge, equally important for the development of a creative attitude is exposure to a "variety of experiences," of points of view, which stimulates experimentation and divergent thinking, making individuals be "more likely to use multiple and diverse perspectives and more complicated schemas" (Shalley and Gilson 2004, p. 36): the "socialization agencies," especially in the stages of primary education, play, as we have seen, a decisive role in putting the learner in a position to exercise such multiple perspectives.

An observation must be made regarding the dimensions of the "fields" of reference and their speed of transformation: in a globalized context, doing something that no one else has done so far is more challenging than before. The field of comparison and the speed with which information arrives from one end of the globe to the other no longer allows anyone to invent things "already invented": competition is on a planetary level. This, instead of mortifying the creative drive in relation to an increasingly unattainable goal (being really an "innovator"), should make us understand, on the contrary, the importance of a widespread culture of creativity in everyday life, the true sociocultural humus that will also allow the emergence of Big C or Historical C products. The fertile ground of creativity is an attitude of openness, regardless of the scope of its results.

I will conclude with a final aspect related to the theme of the development of creative ability, a recent reflection that draws from the past and that is based on the simple observation that when we see behavior in action, we emulate: creativity can be learned with greater success from observation and interaction with "other creatives" than from the possession of an innate ability. According to the "theory of social learning," "to elicit more creativity in followers, followers need to see creativity being exemplified" (Jaussi and Dionne 2003, p. 477), this is because "children develop creativity not when they are told to, but when they are shown how" (Sternberg 2003, p. 126). Gestures are probably the most effective learning tools capable of synthesis, "and can only be learned by participating, imitating, retracing the steps of someone performing them in front of us. Even in traditional analytical teaching this is clear: exercises in logic and mathematics are greatly facilitated by their being learned with a teacher and by social interactions" (Maddalena 2021, p. 58).

This "creative introduction" to reality (through what used to be called a teacher) is perhaps still the most effective dynamic (and at the same time the most disarmed and disarming) to avoid blunting the weapon of knowledge that we still need so much.

References

Andolfi V.R., Di Nuzzo C., Antonietti A. (2017), *Opening the mind through the body: The effects of posture on creative processes*, in "Thinking Skills and Creativity", 24: 20-28.

Arieti S. (1976), *Creativity, The Magic Synthesis*, Basic Books, New York, It. trans. *Creatività. La sintesi magica*, Il Pensiero Scientifico, Roma, 1979.

Austin J.L. (1962), *How to Do Things whit Words*, Clarendon Press, Oxford, trad.it. *Come fare cose con le parole*, Marietti, Genova-Milano, 1987.

Boden M.A. (1998), *Creativity and artificial intelligence*, in "Artificial Intelligence", 103: 347-356.

Boden M.A. (2009), *Creativity: how does it Work?*, in Krausz M., Dutton D., Bardsley K. (ed.), *The Idea of Creativity*, Brill, Leiden-Boston.

Borio G., Garda M. (1989) (ed.), *L'esperienza musicale, teoria e storia della ricezione*, EDT, Torino.

Brewer G.D. (1999), *The challenges of interdisciplinarity*, in "Policy sciences", 32(4), 327-337.

Briskman L. (2009), *Creative Product and Creative Process in Science and Art*, in Krausz M., Dutton D., Bardsley K. (ed.), *The Idea of Creativity*, Brill, Leiden-Boston.

Burgoon J.K. (1991), *Relational Message Interpretations of Touch, Conversational Distance, and Posture*, in "Journal of Nonverbal Behavior", 15 (4), pp. 233-259.

Burleson W. (2005), *Developing creativity, motivation, and self-actualization with learning systems*, in "Int. J. Human-Computer Studies", 63: 436–451.

Csikszentmihalyi M. (2003), *Key Issues in Creativity and Development*, in Sawyer R.K. (2003) *Emergence in Creativity and Development*, in Sawyer R.K., et al., *Creativity and development*, Oxford University Press, New York, pp. 12-60.

Dahrendorf R. (1957), *Soziale Klassen und Klassenkonflikt in der industriellen Gesellschaft*, Köln: Westdeutscher Verlag, It. trans. *Classi e conflitti di classe nella società industriale*, Laterza, Bari, 1963.

Damasio A.R. (1995), *L'errore di Cartesio. Emozione, ragione e cervello umano*, Adelphi Edizioni, Milano.

Dasgupta S. (2003), *Multidisciplinary creativity: the case of Herbert A. Simon*, in "Cognitive Science", 27: 683-707.

Dasgupta S. (2019), *A Cognitive Historical Approach to Creativity*, Routledge, London – New York.

De Masi D. (2003), *La fantasia e la concretezza*, Milano, Rizzoli.

Donati P. (2019), *The Digital Matrix and the Hybridization of Society*, in Ismael Al-Amoudi and Emmanuel Lazega (eds.), *Post-Human Institutions and Organisations: Confronting the Matrix*, Abingdon: Routledge, pp. 67-92.

Feltovich, P.J. – Spiro, R.J. – Coulson, R.L. – Feltovich, J. (1996), *Collaboration within and among minds: Mastering complexity, individually and in groups*, in Koschmann T. (Ed.), *CSCL: theory and practice of an emerging paradigm*, (pp. 25 – 44), Lawrence Erlbaum Associates, Mahwah, NJ.

Ferrarotti F. (1995), *Homo Sentiens,* Liguori, Napoli.

Freud S. (1907/1989), *Creative writers and day-dreaming*, in P. Gay (Ed.), *The Freud reader* (pp. 436–443), New York: Norton.

Fromm E. (1959), *The creative attitude*, in Anderson H.H. (ed.), Creativity and its Cultivation, Harper & Row, New York, It. trans. *La creatività e le sue prospettive*, La scuola, Brescia 1972.

Gil A., Gili G. (2022), *La differenza che arricchisce. Comunicazione e Transculturalità*, Edizioni Santa Croce, Roma.

Gili G., Colombo F. (2012), *Comunicazione, cultura, società: L'approccio sociologico alla relazione comunicativa*, La Scuola, Brescia.

Glăveanu V.P. (2018), *Educating which creativity?*, in "Thinking Skills and Creativity", 27: 25-32.

Glăveanu V.P., et al. (2019), *Advancing Creativity Theory and Research: A Sociocultural Manifesto*, in "The Journal of Creative Behavior", 54(3): 741-745.

Guegan J., Buisine S., Mantelet F., Maranzana N., Segonds F. (2016), *Avatar-mediated creativity: When embodying inventors makes engineers more creative*, in "Computers in Human Behavior", 61: 165-175.

Guilford J.P. (1959), *Characteristic elements of creativity*, in Anderson H.H. (ed.), *Creativity and its Cultivation*, Harper & Row, New York, It. trans. *La creatività e le sue prospettive*, La scuola, Brescia 1972.

Hirsch H.G., Biber-Klemm S., Grossenbacher-Mansuy W., Riem H.H., Joye D., Pohl C., Wiesmann U., Zemp E. (2008), *The Emergence of Transdisciplinarity as a Form of Research*, in A.A.V.V. *Handbook of Transdisciplinary Research*, Springer Verlag, Berlin.

Henriksen D. (2016), *The seven transdisciplinary habits of mind of creative teachers: An exploratory study of award winning teachers,* in "Thinking Skills and Creativity", 22: 212–232.

Hubscher-Younger, T. – Narayanan, H. (2003), *Authority and convergence in collaborative learning*, in "Computers & education", 41: 313-334.

James W. (1884), *What is an emotion?*, in "Mind", 9: 188-205.

James W. (1890), *The Principles of Psychology*, Henry Holt and Company, New York.

Jantsch E. (1970), *Inter- and Transdisciplinary University: A Systems Approach to Education and Innovation*, in "Policy Sciences", 1(4): 403-428.

Jaussi K.S., Dionne S.D. (2003), *Leading for creativity: The role of unconventional leader behaviour*, in "The Leadership Quarterly", 14: 475-498.

Joas H. (1996), *The creativity of action*, Chicago, The University of Chicago press.

Leddy T. (2009), *Creative Interpretation of Literary Texts*, in Krausz M., Dutton D., Bardsley K. (ed.), *The Idea of Creativity*, Brill, Leiden-Boston.

Lubart T. (2008), *Connecting learning, individual differences and creativity*, in "Learning and Individual Differences", 18: 361-362.

Maddalena G. (2015), *The Philosophy of Gesture. Completing Pragmatists' Incomplete revolution*, McGill-Queen's University Press, Montreal & Kingston, London, Chicago.

Maddalena G. (2021), *Filosofia del gesto*, Carocci, Roma.

Maruyama M. (2003), *Causal Loops, Interaction, and Creativity*, in "International Review of Sociology—Revue Internationale de Sociologie", 13(3).

May R. (1959), *The nature of creativity*, in Anderson H.H. (ed.), *Creativity and its Cultivation*, Harper & Row, New York, It. trans. *La creatività e le sue prospettive*, La scuola, Brescia 1972.

McWilliam E., Dawson S. (2008), *Teaching for creativity: towards sustainable and replicable pedagogical practice*, in "High Education" 56: 633-643.

Mead G.H. (1934), *Mind, Self and Society*, Chicago, University of Chicago Press, trad. it. *Mente sé e società*, Giunti, Firenze 1966.

Mead M. (1959), *La Creativity seen from an intercultural perspective*, in Anderson H.H. (ed.), Creativity and its Cultivation, Harper & Row, New York, It. trans. La creatività e le sue prospettive, La scuola, Brescia 1972.

Meheus J., Nickles T. (1999. 2000), *The Methodological Study of Creativity and Discovery – Some Background*, in "Fonduations of Science", 4: 231-235.

Morin E. (2001), *I sette saperi necessari all'educazione del futuro*, Raffaello Cortina Editore, Milano.

Morris D. (1994), *Bodytalk: A World Guide to Gestures*, Jonathan Cape ltd, London, trad. it. *I gesti nel mondo: guida al linguaggio universale*, Mondadori, Milano, 1995.

Nakamura J., Csikszentmihalyi M. (2003), *Creativity in Later Life*, in SAWYER R.K., et al., *Creativity and development*, Oxford University Press, New York, 186-216.

Osborne P. (2015), *Problematizing Disciplinarity, Transdisciplinary Problematics*, in "Theory, Culture & Society", 32(5-6): 3-35.

Paci E. (2004), *Prefazione,* in Merleau-Ponty, M. (1948), *Sens et non-sens,* Nagel, Paris; It. trans. *Senso e non senso. Percezione e significato della realtà,* il Saggiatore, Milano.

Padua D. (2017), *L'azione non-logica paretiana,* in Padua D. (ed.) *La sociologia tra modernità e postmodernità,* Morlacchi Editore, Perugia.

Piaget J. (1971), *The theory of stages in cognitive development,* in Green D.R., Ford M.P. & Flamer G.B. (Eds.), *Measurement and Piaget* (pp. 1–11), New York: Mc-Graw-Hill.

Reiter-Palmon R., Illies J.J. (2004), *Leadership and creativity: Understanding leadership from a creative problem-solving perspective,* in "The Leadership Quarterly", 15: 5- 77.

Reuter M.E. (2015), *Creativity – A Sociological Approach,* Palgrave, London.

Rieff P. (1966), *The Triumph of the Therapeutic: Uses of Faith after Freud,* Harper & Row, New York, It. trans. *Gli usi della fede dopo Freud,* Istituto Librario Internazionale, Milano, 1972.

Sartre J.P. (1947), *Qu'est-ce la littérature?,* Gallimard, Paris, It. trans. *Che cos'è la letteratura?,* Il Saggiatore, Milano, 1995.

Sawyer R.K. (2003), *Emergence in Creativity and Development,* in Sawyer R.K., et al., *Creativity and development,* Oxford University Press, New York, pp. 12-60.

Schütz A. (1951), *Making Music Together: A Study in Social Relationship,* in "Social Research", 18(1): 76-97.

Shalley C.E., Gilson L.L. (2004), *What leaders need to know: A review of social and contextual factors that can foster or hinder creativity,* in "The Leadership Quarterly", 15: 33-53.

Sinnott E.W. (1959), *The creativity of life,* in Anderson H.H. (ed.), *Creativity and its Cultivation,* Harper & Row, New York, It. trans. *La creatività e le sue prospettive,* La scuola, Brescia 1972.

Stanciu M.M. (2015), *Embodied creativity: a critical analysis of an underdeveloped,* in "Procedia - Social and Behavioral Sciences", 187: 312-317.

Sternberg R.J. (2003), *The Development of Creativity as a Decision-Making Process* in Sawyer R.K., et al., *Creativity and development,* Oxford University Press, New York.

Sternberg R.J. (2005), *Creativity or creativities?,* in "Int. J. Human-Computer Studies", 63: 370-382.

Sternberg R.J., Spear-Swerling, L. (1996), *Teaching for Thinking,* American Psychological Association, Washington, D.C.; It. trans. *Le tre intelligenze.*

Come potenziare le capacità analitiche, creative e pratiche, Erickson, Trento 2002.

Sweller J. (2009), *Cognitive Bases of Human Creativity,* Educ. Psychol. Rev. 21, 11-19.

Tsuchiya J. (2022), *Sociological issues of social control and power in information sciences,* in "Metis", XXIX(1-2): 147-174.

Turkle S. (2011), *Alone Together. Why We Expect More from Technology and Less from Each Other,* Basic Books, New York, It. trans. *Insieme ma soli. Perché ci aspettiamo sempre più dalla tecnologia e sempre meno dagli altri,* Codice Edizione, Torino, 2012.

4

Relational Dimension of Creativity

Abstract One of the principal objects of study in sociology is that concerning processes, especially those of a cultural nature: by the term process we are used to denote "sequences of events, that is, changes in structures, which show some degree of regularity, order, direction, tendency" (Strassoldo, *Forma e funzione. Introduzione alla sociologia dell'arte*, 2001, p. 216). In Chap. 3 we have seen which processes are related to the concrete expression, stimulation, and development of that initial move we have called "creative attitude."

We will conclude our analysis with a final summarizing insight to show how the origin (and to some extent, the destiny) of creative energy and the practices aimed at implementing it cannot avoid considering the centrality of the relational dimension: I admit that this is a choice of field, not unanimously shared, but, in my opinion, it is the most effective in identifying sources and objectives of this "eccentric" human potentiality. The principle of "emergence" proposed here complements and completes (and maybe also surpasses) that of "social interdependence" of gestalt derivation for which "the whole is different from the sum of its individual parts." Equally, we can assert that "all creativity is an emergent process that involves a social group" (Sawyer, *Emergence in Creativity and Development*, 2003, p. 19). But the most interesting problem to be solved

© The Author(s) 2024
P. P. Bellini, *The Creative Gesture*, Palgrave Studies in Creativity and Culture,
https://doi.org/10.1007/978-3-031-54219-0_4

is not really that of "cooperation": it is, in fact, prone to an easy reductionism of a merely instrumental nature. Moreover, cooperation is not a specifically and exclusively human element, given that many animals are able to compete with us in this area: "Meerkats, moles, many types of social insects, and even bacteria achieve high levels of cooperation" (Tomasello, *Why we Cooperate*, 2009, It. transl. 2010, p. 118).

Instead, we would like to verify the validity of what Martin Buber "intuited" a century ago, applying new and updated methodologies of inquiry: "In the beginning is the relationship" (Buber, *Rede über das Erzieherische*, 1926, It. transl. 1993, p. 72).

Keywords Relationality • Primary sociality • We-ness • Intercorporeity

4.1   The "Primary Sociality"

As the book draws to a close, it seems appropriate to offer a final personal reflection on the socio-anthropological premises from which I started: talking about creativity today means, indirectly, touching on a topic that delves into the depth of the person and in the construction of their identity. Here I would like to propose a synthetic relational framework, as a key to interpreting the issues dealt with during this investigation of creativity.

To do this, it is useful to establish a hermeneutic starting point that lies at the root of every investigative approach focused on social relationships: the concept of "emergence" is fundamental to adequately understand relationality. With its roots in nineteenth-century organicism, emergence can be defined as the theory "that the organism is different from the sum of its parts and that it depends on the structural arrangement of the parts" (Sawyer 2003, p. 14). From this perspective, every innovation, every change is the result of an organism-environment interaction: in a certain sense, therefore, "all creativity is an emerging process that involves a social group of individuals engaged in complex, unpredictable interactions" (ibid., p. 19).

Starting from this general premise, it can therefore be stated that creative action is, at all times, relational. In fact, there is no form of human creativity that is not based on direct, mediated, or implicit social interactions or exchanges and even when we work in solitude we interact with the opinions, knowledge, and expectations of others: therefore, "the lifelong development of creativity cannot be conceived outside of self-other relations" (Glăveanu et al. 2019, p. 742). To document this "choice of field," I will borrow reflections from three of the many authors cited in this book whose thought seems to me can adequately explain the basic choices that scholars have to face.

I will start with Richard Florida, a world-renowned economist, author of a widely known and substantial volume, *The rise of the creative class* : his broad analysis impeccably illustrates the characteristics, conditions, and properties of creativity that we could define as "winning," effective, characteristic of the rising class, which once was the prerogative of Western Europe (*primarily* Italy) and which in the last century has been monopolized by American culture thanks to the three Ts (Technology, Talent, Tolerance). More or less explicitly, his conception breathes a framing of creativity as the essence of individual realization, as fuel and process of the journey that leads to personal "happiness."

From this perspective, the "relational" dimension of creativity consequently comes to be assigned to a secondary position, a sort of obligatory acceptance and all-in-all instrumental (the "creative community"). The optimal social ecology for the development of creative potential is consequently identified in operational contexts as far away as possible from the "dense human fabric" of the neighborhoods of the past: the communities most suited to favor creative expressiveness are, on the contrary, those characterized "by the precariousness of relationships and by 'loose' ties, which allow us to live the almost anonymous existence that we like and not those imposed by others" (Florida 2002, It. trans. 2003, p. 37).

As can be imagined, this is essentially an attitude of "defense" against relationships that are too solid, "cumbersome" relationships, which are demonstratively considered as obstacles to the full development of creativity. This approach brings out the heart of the underlying option, which presents itself to anyone who wants to face the dynamics related to "ultimate concerns" (as Margaret Archer would define them) that are at the root of any human action: should creativity be considered an "ultimate value" or is it itself justified by a goal that hierarchically precedes it?

These are questions that, clearly, cannot be dissected with analytical methodologies, but that, perhaps for this reason, presuppose a choice of field, explicit or implicit as it may be (the same goes for other strongly connotative terms, such as "freedom," "justice," "good," etc.).

More or less consciously or explicitly, many researchers today are trying to clarify the ways in which individual and social factors combine in the creative process. What inevitably emerges, in this case, is a methodological question: if both the individual and social dimensions are involved, "what is the nature of the relationships and causal connections between these levels?" (Sawyer 2003, p. 50). Florida's *frame* is certainly diametrically opposed to that of Pierpaolo Donati: it is possible to build a situation and even a social system in which everyone gets their own result precisely because of "loose" ties, but all this could happen "at the expense of human relationships and with them we forfeit happiness" (Donati and Solci 2011, p. 210).

I will now move on to a second author I have frequently cited, Alfred Schütz, who, by identifying the keystone of every cultural and anthropological process in the "bond," proposes a fundamentally alternative perspective to that of Florida, starting precisely from the mother relationship of creative action and, therefore, of its purposes. Creativity, for Schütz is a process that finds its original impetus in what he defines as "orientation to the Other": all the experience of social reality is based on the fundamental axiom "that postulates the existence of other beings 'like me,' whose constitution is directly based on the orientation to you" (Schütz and Luckmann 1973, p. 61). Such orientation, it should be clarified, is conceived not as a spontaneous feeling or a moral inclination, but rather as a structural element, anthropological: "As long as man is born of woman, intersubjectivity and the *we-relationship* will be the foundation of all other categories of human existence [...]. Precisely for this reason, everything in human life is founded on the primal experience of the *we-relationship* [...], since all other categories of human existence are founded on the primal experience of being born [...], the fundamental ontological category of human existence in the world and therefore of all philosophical anthropology" (Schütz 1966, p. 82).

In his essay, *Scheler's theory of intersubjectivity and the general thesis of the alter ego*, Schütz emphasized that there is a presupposition taken for granted that no one, not even the most skeptical, doubts even for a moment: "We are simply born into a world of Others. As long as human beings are not concocted like homunculi in retorts but are born and brought by mothers, the sphere of 'We' will be naively presupposed" (Schütz 1962, p. 168). What we all start from for the great leap toward alterity (intersubjectivity, communication) is the "naively presupposed" (therefore also unconscious) fact that we are born, and "born of woman" (a radicality that probably draws from Schütz's Jewish culture and the centrality of the matriarchal line as the source of identity/belonging).

More recently Hans Joas arrives at similar "presuppositions" by another route: the starting point of his analysis draws from Merleau-Ponty's *Phenomenology of Perception*, which considers the relationship of the subject with others in a pre-linguistic sense, in the stage of infant development. At the base of every experience, there would not only be corporeality, but the interrelation between the experience of our body and the experience of the bodies of others, the "*intercorporeity.*" By different paths, the thought of the French philosopher also goes to the care that the mother reserves for the newborn through position, gesture, and voice, "for it is this which enables the infant to advance from his original state of indifferentiation and to relate to the world as a separate ego" (Joas 1996, p. 181).

The observations of Richard Zaner (who studied under Schütz) also draw from the filial relationship to highlight the relational dimensions of creativity: it is the primary experience of being born that makes all of us in some way "debtors" for our being to the Other (mother above all), and therefore responsible, on the one hand, for the recognition of our state and, on the other, for the great enterprise of "becoming ourselves," "which is itself always a task and chore, and even when not always accomplished, done within the nexus of our growing old together" (Zaner 2002, pp. 15 and 17). Yet, strangely, "philosophers have written and chatted, at times incessantly, about death, and have said almost nothing about birth. Why is this?" (ibid., p. 12).

In sociological reflection (which to date, as I have had to acknowledge, has not yet produced a fully mature and satisfactory heuristic model)[1], the "social" dimension of creativity often fails to go beyond a model of external influence, it fails to "see" how creativity occurs within relationships, in the interdependence between Ego and Alter: there is no clash between the two and, even more, "these two 'segments' are not isolated but elements that co-constitute each other" (Glăveanu 2010, p. 84).

Creativity, from this perspective, can only be conceived as a "penultimate good," whose goal is to restore an original and no longer guaranteed relationality (as stated in many of the reflections reported here), to manifest the "primary sociality of all human capacity for action" (Joas 1996, p. 148). Joas, like Schütz, speaks of a "tacit presupposition," so tacit and so presupposed that it would be inscribed even in the very body of humans, a primary sociality not generated by conscious intentionality, but rather precedes it, "a structure of common action which initially consists solely of our interaction with other bodies" (ibid., p. 184).

The third and last author is the philosopher/sociologist Martin Buber, who offers a worthy "creative" conclusion to this academic journey, a transcendental vision, an appropriate synthesis of an educational responsibility, and a deep yet difficult aspiration of the human spirit:

> The instinct of creativity, left to itself, does not lead, cannot lead to two formations indispensable for the construction of a true human life: to participate in a cause and to access reciprocity. Single work and collective work are two very different things. Building something is a pride of being mortal, but being conditioned to a common work, the unconscious humility of being part, of taking part and of having a part is the authentic nourishment of earthly immortality [...]. An education based only on the formation of the instinct of creativity would prepare a new, very painful solitude of man. This is something greater than what the supporters of libido believe: it is desire that the world becomes a person who makes herself present to us, who approaches us as we do her, who chooses us and recognizes us as we do towards her, that she finds confirmation in us as we do in her (Buber 1926, It. trans. 1993, pp. 165 and 166).

---

[1] One of the most convincing recent attempts is perhaps the model proposed by Reuter (2015, p. 57): *The circular social construction of creativity.*

The prophetic tone of this German philosopher could at least induce consideration of the theoretical possibility of an analytical *frame* of creativity that differs from those that dominate today in the sectors of scientific and applicative research: "As long as psychologists find creativity instrumental for our adaptability, self-expression and health, it will continue to attract the interest of both theorists and researchers. But we should remember that creativity also exists beyond psychology" (Glăveanu 2010, p. 91).

Instrumentality is not the final word and not even the most appropriate term with which to describe an energy that inexorably tends to overflow its narrow limits.

4.2   Reflections and Developments

Together we have traveled an articulated, fascinating journey, full of cues and just as many risks: creative capacity, like all things that attract with lures and promises, is capable of defending itself from the attacks of those who would "own" it. It is a youthful energy that seems to indulge those who are young (in defiance of biographical data). It is the energy that allows us to change the world so that it becomes more aligned with the irreducible drive that takes us yonder, beyond the fence of the already done, the already experienced. It is the energy that attests, more than any other, to the inexhaustible human need to overcome the limits of its own nature, of the status quo. And at the same time, it is the synthetic energy that affirms itself by resting its feet on what "has been," without which we could not imagine "what will be." Human existence is a river flowing between the solid banks of stability (within which we are born) and innovation (toward which we are going). Should one of these two banks subside, the river will become a swamp.

Creativity can only be adequately studied through a collaboration of different disciplines: it is a multifaceted energy that has a history, a psychophysical dynamism, a motivational dimension, various developmental practices, various goals, and endless social and cultural conditions. Nowadays, the study of creativity implies a certain willingness to make a "leap," not in a romantic sense, but in a methodological sense: those who do not want to "get their hands dirty" with other perspectives risk seeing their own impoverished as well. And so, even in the specifics of university disciplines, the study of creativity invites the scholar to imagine himself in the original position, that which involves risking the old (always valuable) in the impact with the new (always risky), rebalancing the shoes of the teacher with those of the student, feeling "ignorant" again, while knowing so much. Creativity, which fortunately is more widespread today, with its opportunities and also with its (sometimes pathological) risks, imparts a speed to modern life such as has never recorded before: the current challenges generated by technology impose on research the courage, and also the humility, to find new avenues of inquiry, capable of overcoming the narrowness of disciplines without losing their richness and also utility. Today, a "synthetic" look is not only desirable but essential and can be postponed no longer.

Sociology must do—and is doing, with a partly excusable delay—its part. It could be said that its most significant contribution at the present is "containment": it calls upon aesthetics, psychology, pedagogy, anthropology, philosophy, cognitive sciences, humanistic, and literary studies to come to terms with that "relational" dimension to which I have frequently referred. Everything new is born on the ground of what we have received, there is nothing subjective that is not an "emergent" result of what we have encountered. For if human life takes shape in the social context, this condition carries with it the law of everyday existence: neither totally free nor totally bound. Sociology is a step or two behind: it needs to regain ground. Above all, it must field its ability (and responsibility) to "see" the relationship within human action, something the man in the street forgets to do (and often scientists forget as well): and it must do so by employing its own weapons, which are reflexivity and empirical inquiry (that to date have not been used nearly enough on this issue).

And sociology needs "to become a child again," not in the childish or naïve sense which would not befit a university discipline, but in the sense of not being afraid to intermingle with other disciplines so they will all be to some extent fertilely "contaminated."

References

Buber M. (1926), *Rede über das Erzieherische*, Lambert Schneider, Heilderberg, It. trans. *Il principio dialogico e altri saggi*, Edizioni San Paolo, Milano, 1993.

Donati, P. – Solci, R. (2011), *I beni relazionali. Che cosa sono e quali effetti producono*, Bollati Boringhieri, Torino.

Florida R. (2002), *The rise of the creative class*, Basic Books, New York, It. trans. *L'ascesa della nuova classe creativa*, Mondadori, Milano, 2003.

Glăveanu V.P. (2010), *Paradigms in the study of creativity: Introducing the perspective of cultural psychology*, in "New Ideas in Psychology", 28: 79-93.

Glăveanu V.P., et al. (2019), *Advancing Creativity Theory and Research: A Sociocultural Manifesto*, in "The Journal of Creative Behavior", 54(3): 741-745.

Joas H. (1996), *The creativity of action*, Chicago, The University of Chicago press.

Reuter M.E. (2015), *Creativity – A Sociological Approach*, Palgrave, London.

Sawyer R.K. (2003), *Emergence in Creativity and Development*, in Sawyer R.K., et al., *Creativity and development*, Oxford University Press, New York, pp. 12-60.

Schütz A. (1962), *Scheler's theory of intersubjectivity and the general thesis of the alter ego*, Collected Papers, Vol I The Hague: Martinus Nijhoff.

Schütz A. (1966), *The problem of transcendental intersubjectivity in Husserl*, Collected Papers, III The Hague: Martinus Nijhoff.

Schütz A. and Luckmann T. (1973), *The Structures of Life-Word*, Evanston, Illinois, Northwestern University Press.

Zaner R.M. (2002), *Making Music Together while Growing Older: Further Reflections on Intersubjectivity*, in "Human Studies", 25(1): 1-18.

Index[1]

---

[1] Note: Page numbers followed by 'n' refer to notes.

P. P. Bellini, *The Creative Gesture*, Palgrave Studies in Creativity and Culture, https://doi.org/10.1007/978-3-031-54219-0

GPSR Compliance

The European Union's (EU) General Product Safety Regulation (GPSR) is a set of rules that requires consumer products to be safe and our obligations to ensure this.

If you have any concerns about our products, you can contact us on ProductSafety@springernature.com

In case Publisher is established outside the EU, the EU authorized representative is:

Springer Nature Customer Service Center GmbH
Europaplatz 3
69115 Heidelberg, Germany

FSC
www.fsc.org
MIX
Papier | Fördert
gute Waldnutzung
FSC® C083411

Zeitfracht Medien GmbH
Ferdinand-Jühlke-Straße 7
99095 Erfurt, Deutschland
produktsicherheit@kolibri360.de